LEADING

YOUR TEAM

How to involve and inspire teams

Second edition

Andrew Leigh &
Michael Maynard

NICHOLAS BREALEY
PUBLISHING

LONDON

To our team who forgive our failings and keep encouraging us to do even better

THE SURREY INSTITUTE OF ART & DESIGN

This second edition published by
Nicholas Brealey Publishing in 2002

First published in 1995

3–5 Spafield Street
Clerkenwell, London
EC1R 4QB, UK
Tel: +44 (0)20 7239 0360
Fax: +44 (0)20 7239 0370

1163 E. Ogden Avenue, Suite 705-229
Naperville
IL 60563-8535, USA
Tel: (888) BREALEY
Fax: (630) 898 3595

http://www.nbrealey-books.com

ISBN 1-85788-304-7

British Library Cataloguing in Publication Data
A catalogue record for this book is available from the British Library.

Printed in Finland by WS Bookwell

Contents

Acknowledgements

We would like to thank the following for their comments and contributions:

Nicholas Brealey, our publisher, for challenging us to go the whole way; our colleagues in Coopers and Lybrand (now PricewaterhouseCoopers), including Richard Killick, Claire Belfield, and Neil Lazenbury for sharing his wisdom and experience about leading multicultural teams; colleagues in Allied Dunbar Assurance include Steve Hutable, Paul Lewis and Jane McCann; Sue Petitt of Sun Alliance; David Cleeton of Wimberry Management Development and Training for his early insightful and detailed analysis; Caroline Doughty of Laura Ashley; Stuart MacKenzie of MLA for again reminding us about our aspirations; Nigel Hughes, Martin Cochrane and Michaela Justice of MLA; Bernard Sullivan of Rover; and Sally Lansdell for her expert help with the manuscript. Special thanks to Ian Cutler at KPMG Financial Services for his advice and comments on virtual teams, also thanks to Rohan Garnett, British Airways, Richard Gilder at Dell, Chris Collison of BP Amoco and Jo Sovin for research support.

Sources include: *Best Practice* magazine, January 1994, IFS International Ltd; *Bulletpoint* magazine (various issues), published by Bulletpoint Communications Ltd; the bell-shaped agenda structure in Chapter 2 is adapted from an idea by John E. Tropman in *Effective Meetings*, Sage Publications, Inc. (1981); '10 ways leaders manage the future' in Chapter 12 is adapted from an idea by Warren Bennis in *On Becoming a Leader*, Hutchinson Books (1989); Kawal S Banga, unpublished MSc dissertation on the use of Belbin team roles (September 1993); the two diagrams in Chapter 13 were adapted from material in *Mind Your Manners* by John Mole, Nicholas Brealey Publishing (1996) and *Riding the Waves of Culture* by Fons Trompenaars, Nicholas Brealey Publishing (1997); material on Imagination in Chapter 12 was adapted from *Human Resources* magazine, Autumn 1994.

Most of all we would like to acknowledge the support and understanding of our respective families. They are our hidden team members, and without them the book would not exist.

Introduction to the Second Edition

What kind of team leader do you want to be? Successful obviously, yet what will it take to have a group of people really rooting for your aims, willing to go that extra mile, and doing things that surprise and delight you and your colleagues?

Leading Your Team is a distillation of team wisdom, drawn from many sources, including our own experience of working in and advising many different kinds of teams. In our development and consulting company we are passionate about the power of teams and the importance of leading by example. So *Leading Your Team* is no theoretical treatise, it stems from the reality of making teams work in many diverse settings.

This second edition retains the basic structure of the original version because the concepts remain important, whether it is how to run an inspired team meeting or staying adaptable. If anything, the issues identified in the first edition have become even more important to being a successful team leader.

We have added a new chapter on virtual teams since many team leaders will be faced with at least one of these, either as a participant or as a group that they must facilitate and inspire. Since we run a virtual team in our company we know from daily experience how powerful such groups can be. It is not so much the technology that matters as the way in which new forms of relationships are able to generate far more than the sum of the parts. And that, after all, is what team work is all about.

Being a team leader can be immensely satisfying, yet also incredibly frustrating. If management is getting things done, leadership is often providing direction and then getting out of the way. In a team you are often judged less by what you can personally achieve than by how you let others do what they are able to do.

Team leadership is also far more than a technical challenge of coordination and project management. It is essentially a test of character. You seldom have the sort of authority that allows you simply to instruct people and expect them to perform obediently. Even the armed forces have started to abandon that approach faced with the complexity of talents and know-how that modern fighting demands.

What sort of person do you need to be to lead a team successfully? We believe you will be someone who welcomes responsibility while also knowing how to fire it up in other people. You are likely to be a proactive person with a positive attitude to life that infects your relationships with other people. In other words, you are a chooser rather than a victim.

In our work in companies at all levels of organisations, we commonly find a distinction between victims and choosers. The former blame others, are reactive and spend time moaning and therefore demotivating others around them. Strangely, we have met plenty of people in positions of authority who repeatedly behave as victims. They seldom make good team leaders.

Choosers, on the other hand, are proactive, continually seeking to improve and demonstrate a 'can

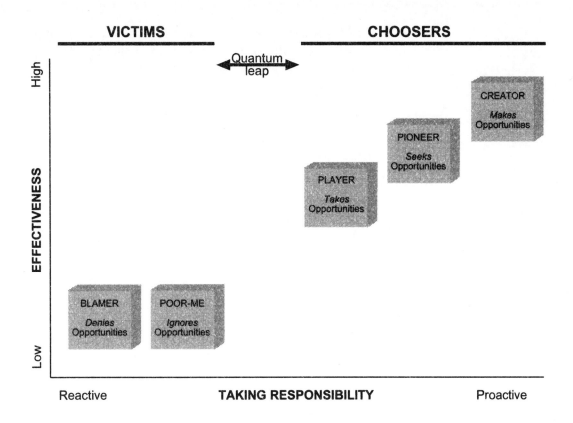

do' attitude that influences all those with whom they come into contact. Most of all, choosers make things happen.

Interestingly, the best leaders we meet seem to be choosers committed to continually developing themselves. That is, they actively try to move from being *players* who simply take opportunities, to being *pioneers* who seek opportunities, to becoming *creators* who make opportunities. For this you need to be highly self-aware and concerned with how you affect others. In other words, you need a high emotional intelligence.

Emotional intelligence, unlike conventional IQ, can be continually improved over time. So good team leaders are never really satisfied with their own performance and always push to grow their capability at leading groups. As team leaders ourselves we are only too aware of how often we get it wrong and of how much our team has to teach us. If you regard your team as a teacher you will probably never go far wrong in leading your group towards its common goal.

Survival Kit 1

So you want to lead a team? People are expecting you to lead. How do you do it, and do it superbly?

Leadership is now high on your personal agenda. Perhaps you are wondering, 'Do I have what it takes?' The answer is almost certainly 'yes'. You can lead a team, and do it successfully, through a mixture of knowledge, practice and risk taking.

You are certainly not alone if you are wondering where to start. Many people are thrown in at the deep end and simply told to get on with it. Often they are given daunting new responsibilities, virtually without warning.

It may not even be new responsibilities that concern you. It could be that your biggest worry is how to handle people who were previously your peers, even your friends. How will they respond to your exercising authority — how do you strike a balance between being still friendly, yet also conveying the clear message that you are the leader?

Or perhaps your biggest headache is how to handle the experts. A few years ago in many organisations, leaders had a treasury of knowledge or skill to draw on. They could convincingly use it to impress others. Today you are just as likely to find yourself leading experts with far more knowledge than you, or who are far more up to date. If that is not true now, it almost certainly will be in three or four years' time.

The rest of this book is designed to help you handle such challenges.

You short-change yourself and team members by only aiming for average performance. Going for a superb team will inspire you, and contribute to inspiring others. It will stimulate everyone into thinking more creatively about what it will take to succeed.

When a cast of professional actors meets to stage a play, for example, everyone is excited and energised at the prospect. They all want to produce something outstanding, not run of the mill. The director takes for granted the collective wish to excel. The cast too assumes that the director wants excellence. The main scope for disagreement is usually about how to achieve this exceptional performance.

In business organisations, the requirement for the leader to help the team excel is less common. Frequently, team leaders themselves admit that just being competent is enough for them. Yet only by reaching for the stars can you hope to encourage others to do the same.

WHAT PRICE THEORIES?

Even if you have been well prepared for leadership, the prospect can still seem overwhelming. There is a chasm between leadership theories and doing the actual job. It would be understandable if by now you feel the need for some kind of survival kit.

Most theories and models of leadership tend to be descriptive, rather than prescriptive. They rarely explain how to do the job. It is fine being told to be adaptable, to communicate, to set objectives, yet how exactly are you supposed to do that with your particular team?

Theories and models can provide a useful route map, planting signposts to watch for along the way. Yet most effective leaders start with a vision, rather than a theory. They learn on the job, acquiring bits of theory later. For

example, we start the 'how to' part of this book not with
theory but with a chapter on how to run an inspired team
meeting. In our experience this is usually more
immediately useful to practising team leaders than
plunging straight into the intricacies of ideas such as
'situational leadership' or 'Theory Y'.

" The old (and still pervasive) dictum says that the job of
the manager is to tell people what to do. My research says
that the manager's job is to lead. **"**
(Robert Waterman)

The logical route to tackling the leadership job might be
first to understand the theory, move to strategy and from
there go to the more mundane aspects of the work. In
practice it is a more complicated road to travel. As
Warren Bennis, one of the most respected leadership
theorists puts it, 'the process of becoming a leader is
much the same as the process of becoming an integrated
human being.'

To succeed in leading teams, you are signing on for a
lifelong voyage of personal exploration. Forget 'outward
bound', you are embarking on an 'inward bound' journey
of incredible challenge. One of the biggest requirements
is to use your self-expression to the full.

"Increasingly people will follow only those who
demonstrate a willingness and an ability to accommodate
their needs, and the tools of fear, social position and the
like will be less available. A different paradigm for
leadership is needed. **"**
(Geoff Keeys,
Director of Personnel and Business Services,
Prudential Corporation plc)

Talking point

WHAT PEOPLE EXPECT OF THEIR LEADERS

American executives who have been asked 'What do you look for and admire in your leaders?' have produced strikingly consistent answers over seven years of surveys:

- Honest   87%
- Competent   74%
- Forward looking   67%
- Inspiring   61%
- Intelligent   46%
- Fair-minded   42%
- Broad-minded   38%
- Courageous   35%
- Straightforward   33%
- Imaginative   32%
- Dependable   31%

Source: Establishing the Credibility Factor, *Best Practice* magazine, January 1994.

Leaders are always people who are able to express themselves fully, whether in public meetings, team briefings or in one-to-one encounters. There is also evidence that the people who most succeed in organisational life tend to be those best able to communicate and use their self-expression.

So it makes sense for Chapter 3 to deal with team briefings. Research in mid-1994 by the Industrial Society, involving 1000 managers, rated this the best method for communicating with staff and hearing their views.

MADE NOT BORN

Talk to successful leaders and they will usually agree on two basic points. First, that most leaders are made not born. Leaders are produced more by their own efforts than by anything their organisation does to or for them. Secondly, successful leaders are seldom interested in leading for its own sake. They are not driven, they drive.

They are less concerned with proving themselves or being the centre of attention than in expressing themselves and making something happen.

BEING A SUCCESSFUL TEAM LEADER IS

- Taking responsibility for the team's performance
- Being yourself
- Developing a guiding purpose that excites you and others
- Persistently pursuing your guiding purpose
- Expanding your own self-expression
- Listening to your inner voice
- Learning from those who can help you
- Making things happen that you care about
- Not ascribing success or failure to external circumstances nor taking sole credit for it

You cannot learn how to lead or inspire people solely from books, any more than you can become a fine presenter by reading about speech making. You will mainly learn through practical experience. However, knowledge of some of the basics can be acquired through reading, coaching and other less direct methods.

By themselves, our suggestions on how to lead are merely a list of possibilities. They have to be welded into your own personal approach and style. For this you need to make yourself open to two vital creative forces: other people, and experimentation.

Being open to people is a mixture of good listening, responding with empathy, showing your own vulnerability, and valuing differences. How you react to ideas, for instance, quickly shows whether or not you are open to people and what they have to say.

Openness to experimentation is the other sure way to improve your chance of leading well. Every successful business, for example, is really a group of people discovering what to do as they go along. The idea that 'we now know the rules' is probably one of the most dangerous and misleading beliefs an organisation can acquire. The history of IBM in the late 1980s and early 1990s shows how destructive it can be.

Experimentation also means crossing all kinds of boundaries — your own, the team's, the department's, the organisation's. Your team has to discover how it can best produce outstanding results. For this it requires information from customers, suppliers, colleagues, managers, and so on. Only when you start acting on the information and putting it to work will you discover what it really means.

So the better teams, and the more inspiring team leaders, are always testing assumptions, checking their current perception of reality against real results. Yet teams, like organisations, tend towards a natural inertia. Testing may gradually cease or become too limited. This is another reason why your leadership is so important. You are a vital force for stimulus and encouragement, sustaining the constant process of testing and experimentation.

YOU AS A LEADER

What sort of leader do you want to be? Do you currently have a mental picture of how to get others to do what you want? For example, you may feel that the best way is to take total responsibility for everything the team does, including all the decisions. Do that and you will probably spend most of your time controlling, directing and delegating. That is certainly one well-tried way on which many managers rely entirely.

Leaders with a passion for control, though, seem to become less viable almost by the day. It perpetuates a 'them and us' divide. Nor is it appropriate for leading many kinds of modern teams. Those of today and certainly tomorrow are likely to be less hierarchical, often temporary and complex.

For instance, project teams are frequently created by drawing together people from different parts of an organisation and even beyond it. It is increasingly necessary to form teams of experts from competing organisations, who must learn to collaborate.

In the public sector the challenge is often to create new teams of previously disparate, even competing interests. For example, health workers must collaborate with social services departments if community care is ever to become a reality. Loosely coordinated local government departments must create new multidisciplinary teams to provide a more integrated, customer-sensitive service.

DOCTORS AS LEADERS

Doctors too must learn to lead. Many Primary Health Care Teams face great pressure to become real teams instead of teams only in name.

In the Medway area of Kent, a local group of doctors and other health workers have attempted systematically to develop stronger teams. In their studies they discovered that the GP was held to be the most important member of the team, with the Community Nurse coming a close second.

In such teams the expectation is that the doctor will do the leading. However, the nature of medical training is more likely to create a controlling than a supportive leader. Yet many members of the Primary Health Care Team owe no direct allegiance to the GP. In the large Gun Lane practice, for example, several doctors share the services of nearly 20 separate support staff, ranging from receptionists to social workers and health visitors.

To improve their services many GPs are realising that there is a limit to what they can achieve alone. The role of teamwork and hence their role as leader are becoming more central.

The prospect of working in a team where the leader mainly relies on control and formal authority is also proving unattractive to a growing number of employees. The ones most likely to resist are those with professional, technical or specialist skills. People's expectations about how they want to be led are changing. Today's leaders realise that you have to give up control to get results. An alternative to being a controlling, directing type of leader is to become a supportive, empowering leader. This is someone who enables, inspires and shares responsibility with the team. When you choose to rely on being supportive rather than controlling, success comes through sharing your leadership and power.

You cannot empower someone else without helping them. This means you become concerned to develop them as human beings, to assist with their growth and development. This implies an understanding of the difference between controlling people and controlling results. When you stop trying to supervise people you have more time for discovering what they need to be effective.

The focus on individual performance needs to be matched by one on team performance as a whole. Today's and tomorrow's leaders must learn to drive performance across the entire team, both by utilising individual potential and by creating a team that is more than the sum of its parts.

NO ONE BEST WAY

Much of the information widely available about leading teams seems to imply there is one 'best' way of doing it. For example, built into many of the suggestions found in training packs and courses are certain narrow cultural assumptions. Today's and tomorrow's leaders, however, may be working with people not only from different organisations which have their own, unique way of doing things, but also with people and teams drawn from several nationalities. Gender differences too can often be a hidden factor influencing how the team performs.

That there is no single best way of leading a team should be obvious, yet busy, practising leaders naturally want tools and techniques that work. The suggestions throughout this book do not claim to be culturally neutral or universal in their application. They are ultimately suggestions that effective leaders will build into their personal portfolios of skills as appropriate.

If there is such a thing as a universal message behind our suggestions for leading and inspiring a team, it is about the importance of trying to understand the team and keeping on learning and experimenting. There remains an inevitable tension between the controlling, directing form of leadership and the helping, supportive kind mainly described in this book. While we believe the latter is a more viable approach, each person must find their own balance between these two ways of leading.

In practical terms, there are fewer people these days with the time to control. The death of middle management has cut such a swathe through so many organisations that often facilitating leadership is the only viable way to achieve anything.

GOALS

Supportive leaders never abandon control. Instead they focus it on results, through helping people perform at their best. They give careful attention to how objectives are chosen. Hence Chapter 4 is on setting inspired goals.

66 The role of the manager in the future is going to be to support and coach the experts who are doing the work. 99
(Geoff Shingles, Chairman of Digital Equipment Company)

Across the world, team leaders suffer from a common failing. This is a reluctance or perhaps inability to help their team set clear and uplifting goals. In the 1960s and 1970s the passion for management by objectives tried to address this issue and failed. It was rejected as bureaucratic, inflexible and over-controlling. The resulting vacuum has been filled with a queue of other panaceas, from total quality management to the latest favourite solution, whatever that happens to be.

Viewed from our own experience of leading and advising on teams, and the considerable body of international research now available, goal setting remains one of the most critical leadership tasks. In an era of supportive rather than controlling leadership the approach to goals must alter. The shift is to more involvement, in some cases to situations that leave goal creation almost entirely to others.

To help your team arrive at inspiring goals, you will need to spend time listening, questioning, building agreement, offering participation in decision making and releasing people's full potential. There is less scope or even necessity to be directive on every matter.

A true test of an effective leader is not whether you ensure goal setting occurs, but whether you make it positively inspiring. Inspirational goals get people out of bed in the morning and induce them to come to work on time, or even to take that extra step to achieve the goal by staying late or working at weekends.

PRODUCTIVITY

The shift from controlling to supporting leadership is virtually irreversible. It reflects a widespread realisation that the old ways have not always worked well, and recognition that other pressures are making this the only way to go.

For example, the need to form strategic alliances with competitors, suppliers and customers makes the controlling type of leadership less workable. Employees are also voting with their feet. In a recessionary economy the message is heard loudest from those with a particular expertise, technical ability or professional training. These people seem to flourish better in a supportive environment. As economies move out of recession others too will have a greater choice.

The drive towards a more supportive form of leadership at the expense of control is embodied in the worldwide movement to introduce self-managing teams. Begun in the early 1960s by Procter and Gamble in America, these led to such dramatic increases in productivity that at first they were a closely guarded secret.

Today the secret is out. People perform better when they have control over their lives and particularly their work. Visit the production line of LandRover, for example, and you will find people working in teams led by someone who has no real authority over them except through their leadership skills.

Given this major trend that few team leaders dare ignore, we make self-managing teams the subject of Chapter 5.

TEAM DEVELOPMENT

Whether the team is self-managed or not, it still needs leadership. As already suggested, the best kind of leader will usually understand how teams develop and how best to support them through their natural evolution.

While each team is unique, unless it experiences certain stages of growth it may never be outstanding. Since supportive team leaders know they cannot directly control these stages, they need to be aware of how to influence them.

What makes the various stages so important are the implications for getting the best from people. Chapter 6 therefore helps you understand the team life cycle and how you might support its natural development.

Successful team leaders are not interested in a team's stage of development for its own sake. They want this information to formulate strategies for dealing with weaknesses and making the best use of team strengths. This means obtaining regular information on how the team is doing, to assess whether it is effective or not.

Traditional ways of measuring a team's success seldom provide information quickly enough to be useful. By the time bottom-line data such as return on capital, annual profits or yearly sales arrives, the leader already knows whether or not the team is succeeding.

Even monthly productivity figures may say little about whether a particular team is working to its full potential. For example, the quality movement assumes that teams have an almost unlimited capacity to keep improving, to find an endless list of changes and innovations.

Alert team leaders therefore need ways of regularly reviewing how the team is doing, each time with sufficient new information to enable them to take decisive action. Chapter 7 introduces a practical way of reviewing a team, using a simple structure for making sense of what is happening.

SOMETHING SPECIAL

A formal team review often shows that performance could be considerably better. Often reality strikes first, by placing a sudden, huge pressure on the team to raise its whole game. At some time most leaders want to extract a heroic team effort.

This is when some controlling leaders really come into their own. The legendary conductor Herbert von Karajan was a total dictator, yet he repeatedly extracted stunning performances from his orchestras. In the business world, the equally legendary Harold Geneen of ITT exercised masterly control through an obsession with detail. He regularly took home at night whole suitcases of reports, returning the next day having read them and prepared to initiate action.

However, these people are the exceptions. Such obsessive leaders also have a record of being overtaken by events. They get away with their extreme behaviour through the urgency of the situation, the power of their personality, sheer professionalism and an equally vital ability to inspire people to reach for greatness. They may survive while the heroic effort is required but, like Winston Churchill after the second world war, they may well later be rejected.

Chapter 8 looks at the implications for supportive leaders of extracting a heroic team response.

PROBLEM PEOPLE

No leader succeeds with absolutely everyone. Even if the team is well managed and has inspiring goals, there are always some people who may reject what is on offer.

Every successful team leader therefore learns how to handle difficult people, although as we explain in Chapter 9, the real issue is not so much the person as their behaviour. It is easy to confuse the two.

Employment legislation and changing organisational expectations pose increasing barriers to leaders who prefer control to offering support. For example, while the simplest solution might simply be to fire a difficult team member, this route is often closed, because it will take too long, or the person does not even report directly to the team leader, or their expertise is essential.

JUDGING THE LEADER

A growing number of organisations are discovering the power of asking team members to judge the effectiveness of the leader.

Companies such as Federal Express ask employees to comment annually on their respective team leaders. People answer around 30 questions, the first 10 of which produce the company's 'leadership index'.

The company sets a baseline for performance and those who fail to reach it must improve. They are reviewed again within six months. Over-controlling leaders do not survive long in such an environment.

INTER-TEAM WORKING

Even if you get all your team members working well, their joint success will almost certainly still depend on how they relate to and deal with other teams. These may be both internal or external teams.

For large companies, creating strategic alliances is an accepted way of dealing with an increasingly competitive environment. To bid for one of the world's largest outsourcing contracts, for example, the fast-growing Computer Sciences Corporation (CSC) teamed up with IBM. To try and regain its once powerful hold on the personal computer market, IBM in turn teamed up with the much smaller Apple Corporation.

Likewise, to undertake the Channel Tunnel, or the new British national lottery, consortia of potential rivals have temporarily abandoned competition in favour of collaboration. In these situations inter-team working is essential, often crossing important cultural barriers.

In smaller organisations inter-team working is just as vital. The scale may be different, yet this approach is often the best way for smaller enterprises to survive and compete with larger rivals.

The exact ground rules for achieving good inter-team working remain to be established. There is less doubt about the need for clear and supportive leadership in such teams. Thus in Chapter 10 we explore how you might encourage inter-team working.

BEING ADAPTABLE

All the above describes some of the important territory which leaders need to explore. It would be wrong to give the impression that supportive leaders are one brand of person and controlling ones another. In practice, successful leaders are a unique mixture of both.

Your challenge as a team leader is to create your own mixture that works for you and your particular team. This mixture may need to alter with each new team you lead. In essence, your success depends on how you adapt your approach.

Adaptable leaders are not necessarily those without principles or personal certainties. They are people who try hard to avoid arrogance and a closed mind to new possibilities. They value creativity and recognise the importance of constant renewal and growth — personal, team and organisational.

Being an adaptable leader, while still holding strongly to certain values and a clear vision, is probably the hardest part of doing the job. Chapter 11 explores how you might develop this adaptability.

You definitely cannot do this leadership job on your own. In fact, one of the many definitions of a leader is someone who has followers. You need your team, sometimes more than they need you. You are more likely to succeed by recognising your total dependence on them. Without their commitment, enthusiasm and willingness to sail in uncharted waters, you are a leader only in name.

For new team leaders, this dependence is one of the most difficult realities to confront. Until now, perhaps you have been able to achieve a great deal on your own, maybe occasionally working with others yet not utterly dependent on them. As a team leader you give up this independence. You need these people, in ways you may not even suspect right now.

Dependency does not imply you are powerless. It does mean you cannot entirely rely on a formal position in the organisation's hierarchy to produce excellent results.

TO TEAM OR NOT TO TEAM

Do you really want a team? Many organisations attempt to establish team working without fully realising some of the cultural implications and what must be given up in exchange. For example, if your company is wedded to individuals competing with each other and being paid for their individual efforts, an effective team system will eventually also demand a shift towards team rewards. Or if you or your company are firmly wedded to maintaining strong hierarchies, then before adopting team working principles it is worth reviewing the implications for the hierarchy system.

Nor are teams a panacea. In many cases when you lead a group of people it may make perfect sense to continue treating them mainly as separate individuals, rather than artificially trying to weld them into a more cohesive team unit. Part of the responsibility of a leader is deciding the best approach.

The work that a team does consists of contributions from everyone on it. Their ability to do this depends on how you arrange their responsibilities, including their workload. A common assumption in leading teams is that everything has to be tackled as a team issue. In practice, many tasks and challenges are best handled either by an individual working alone, or perhaps a small sub-group of the main team. The trick is to decide what work belongs to which. This ability to divert work to where it is best done is one of the secrets of harnessing a team's collective power.

An additional problem for certain companies is how to manage the creative team — a team whose main purpose is to produce a creative solution. Such teams pose special challenges in extracting the best from people.

We explore these issues further in Chapter 12.

MULTICULTURAL TEAMS

Factors such as the development of the European Single Market, the emergence of global companies and fast communication systems are increasingly leading to the creation of teams that cross national and international boundaries. Rather than just French, American, Spanish or German teams, we are seeing multicultural teams emerging.

Multicultural teams pose their own brand of challenges for team leaders. Although there has been an increasing amount of research into cultural diversity, there is still much to do in teasing out the lessons from leadership. In Chapter 13 we present some of the dilemmas and offer a survival guide.

TEAM CHARACTERISTICS

From our many discussions with developers and human resource advisers, we are aware that many are deeply concerned with the limitations of their present ways of making sense of teams and helping them perform better.

The complexity and multidimensional nature of teams are seldom acknowledged. Yet we have noted a growing frustration with the simplistic view of teams. Among other things, this possibly explains why there has been a gradual decline in relying on outward bound solutions for creating teams and developing team leaders.

The more astute organisational developers and leaders recognise that in our fast-moving society, producing effective teams and their leaders demands new ways of thinking. During our consulting work we make many presentations to organisations about teams. We are struck by how steadfastly some refuse to acknowledge the creative dimension of teams, for example, until some radical change in the marketplace forces them to rethink.

For years the most popular way of exploring how to help teams succeed, certainly management teams, was by reviewing team roles. While roles are certainly important, they remain only one dimension. As important is how team members choose to work together — their processes.

In recent years the rise of process consulting has created an important resource on which companies can draw. Indeed, many internal trainers and human resource professionals are learning to turn themselves into process consultants serving their own organisations. Likewise, every leader is essentially the team's own process consultant. This focus on how the team is working together, rather than role analysis, is explored briefly in Chapter 14.

STRATEGIC OVERVIEW

Not everyone will agree with the order in which we have presented the various leadership issues. Some may prefer to start with an even more strategic view than this first chapter presents. Chapter 15 therefore offers a broader picture. It views the leadership task from various perspectives, those of trainers, consultants, team members, policy makers and so on.

Finally, in Chapter 16 we offer 20 basic team tips that have stood the test of time. Though they work, they do not pretend to be all you need to know about leading successful teams. That takes merely a lifetime.

If there is a single factor determining whether or not you succeed or fail with your adventure in team

leadership it is summarised as: '*keep your eye on the ball.*'
While we hope this book will inspire some good
intentions and some practical steps on your part, the
reality is that not much will happen unless what you do is
sustained and reviewed continuously.

Rather than ploughing through the whole book, take a
section at a time and implement some of the ideas. That
way you are more likely to have the energy and scope to
make something new occur.

Inevitably other demands will get in the way of your good
intentions about leading and inspiring your team. Often you
will feel you are doing just fine and can simply relax about
leading. You will doubtless conclude occasionally that with
all the other pressures facing you there is no space for yet
one more team review. If you did not face these kinds of
pressures you would not be the sort of person who takes on
the responsibility of leading a team.

Now is the time to face up to these blocks to better
leadership. Even before you read the rest of this book,
make a commitment to review some of the material and
ideas on a specific date in six months' time. Grab your
diary now and put a date in it to remind yourself.

Despite all the pressures for your attention, nothing
will cost you so dear as taking your attention off your
team. Allow this to occur and some or all of the following
will happen:

- People will feel neglected, unrecognised and unfulfilled
- Unresolved conflicts will break out when you least
  expect them
- Relationships will deteriorate and affect performance
- Work will be done poorly and people will leave —
  either actually or in terms of their commitment

The cost of recruiting a replacement team member is
usually high and the price paid for losing a customer even
higher. Both are common occurrences when leaders allow
their attention to wander too far from their team. Save
yourself and your organisation a great deal of time,
money and personal energy by staying awake — set that
diary date now.

What is

A GROUP ?

A TEAM ?

Shared values
Interdependence
Feelings expressed
Commitment
Interpersonal skills
Consistency
Intensity
Trust
Conflict resolution
Listening
Consensus
Cooperation
Focus on group processes

WEAK

STRONG

2 How to Run an Inspired Team Meeting

In this chapter:

- Well-organised meetings
- Chairing
- Regularity
- Goals
- Participation
- Modelling good behaviour
- Energy
- Agendas
- Minutes and time keeping
- Staying on track
- Handling interruptions
- Inspired meetings
- Monitoring

Is your team heading for a thrombosis? The heart of a healthy team is its meetings, and these need to be strong and vigorous for it to survive. A team exists as a single entity during meetings when it truly comes alive. If there is no hardening of the arteries, you may experience that intangible and mysterious factor, 'teamwork'.

Sports teams continually play and practise together, developing their teamwork. A theatre team constantly rehearses. But business and organisational teams consist of individuals who usually function separately, meeting occasionally.

A business team most obviously functions together during its meetings. This is when continual communication and full joint working occur. It's a precious, important time.

Successful team meetings seldom happen by chance. Even when a team starts with good meetings, these can rapidly deteriorate, as can the quality of the team. This happens to many regular company board meetings, for example, where sheer repetition may create a ritual activity of paper shuffling.

Team meetings need to be creative, enlivening experiences. Ideally, people leave feeling energised, their commitment strengthened. Occasionally meetings should be genuinely inspiring. It is part of your role as leader to make this happen.

Advice points

ASK YOUR TEAM FOR HELP
● What do they think of team meetings? ● Do they have ideas on making meetings enlivening? ● How can we make meetings creative and productive?

WELL-ORGANISED MEETINGS

Because meetings are time consuming and expensive, many people dislike them. Seek your team's help to make them thoroughly organised. Early in the life of a new team, devote time to exploring how to achieve this. It's an investment everyone will appreciate.

All members are responsible for making meetings work well, not just you. For instance, consider asking someone else to handle agenda creation, or the publication of the results. Could someone other than you become responsible for preventing interruptions? Perhaps another team member could act as a timekeeper?

WELL-ORGANISED MEETINGS

- Someone leads, chairs or supports
- Prompt starts
- Focused discussion — people stick to the subject
- Clear purpose or agenda
- Agreed procedures
- Time limited — usually a maximum of 90 mins
- Good preparation
- Effort to reach conclusions via consensus
- Discussion of relevant matters
- Few interruptions
- Everyone can contribute
- Regular summarising
- Good listening
- End on time
- Rapid publication of results and further action

CHAIRING

Somebody, not necessarily the team leader, needs to take responsibility for the way each meeting progresses. People usually expect the leader to do this job, yet many teams work perfectly well with someone else doing it. It is more important always to have one named person who holds the ring, ensuring a productive use of time. Left to themselves, meetings can rapidly deteriorate into time-wasters. For example, there may be good reason to meet occasionally and brainstorm, chew over ideas and experiences, without immediate concern for performance or action. Yet allowing most of your team meetings to degenerate into talking shops soon creates considerable frustration.

If you do not enjoy chairing meetings yet are concerned about letting one other person do it regularly, try rotating the responsibility across all team members. Everyone then discovers how tough it is to run an effective meeting. When it is not their turn, they are more likely to support the person who is chairing. This also allows each person to develop their chairing skills and improve the overall quality of meetings.

Avoid allowing team meetings to become one-way affairs, where you talk and others mainly listen. This is not your chance to dominate, or to show who is in charge, or to order people around. If you see your role as managing the entire meeting you could be relying too much on old-style, controlling leadership. Instead, see the job as acting more like a coach or a guide.

For a more traditional, controlling leader this may seem radical stuff. Who, you may ask, is really in charge? This is the wrong question, since there may be no dispute about who is technically responsible. The real issue is how to make the event worthwhile for everyone.

Alert team leaders devote time to learning about how groups actually work, understanding group processes. They also develop their own ways of encouraging. Suppose, for example, your group decides to brainstorm. Your job is to show people how to do it, to stimulate them to produce ideas, not bombard them with your own.

Ensure team meetings occur regularly, such as once a week, or maybe twice a month. Regular get-togethers are not a luxury. They are an essential part of success. When team members like each other and the work is going well, fewer but highly productive meetings may be possible. When the team fails to provide a sense of belonging, people become alienated and unwilling to accept responsibility for the group's success.

REGULARITY

GOALS

Improve the chance of a successful meeting by making sure everyone is clear about its purpose. Effective team meetings generally focus on goals and performance. Poor meetings often reflect excessive time for sharing information, rather than taking decisions and making them happen.

While all team meetings are partly about information exchange, you can quickly destroy their effectiveness by spending too much time on this. There are plenty of ways to ensure information reaches people without clogging up regular team meetings.

Use regular team meetings to make important choices, plan, and problem solve.

Advice points

AT FORMAL TEAM MEETINGS REGULARLY REVIEW

Goals

● How are we doing with our goals and targets?
● What do we need to do next?

and

Working practices

● How well are we working together?
● What stops us being more effective?
● How might we increase our effectiveness?

These five questions are all concerned with **action**.

PARTICIPATION

A common question posed by team leaders is 'how do I get everyone to participate fully?' For example, what do you do about people who seldom talk or contribute?

Even if you can insist that people attend your meetings, it is still rather like taking a horse to water — you cannot always make them behave exactly as you want. If people do not take part, your meetings are not yet sufficiently encouraging for them to do so.

It can be frustrating to wait for someone to contribute. Give people time to think and prepare themselves for speaking. If you rush them, they may start speaking and grind to an early, embarrassed halt.

By staying alert and tuned to how people are reacting, you are better able to decide when it is appropriate to encourage someone to speak. Often they will give visible signs of wanting to say something by shaking their heads, nodding, frowning, smiling, looking puzzled and so on. Only if you watch for these signals can you act on them.

GETTING PEOPLE TO CONTRIBUTE

- Check for any feelings preventing people from participating
- Put team members in pairs or threes to discuss an issue
- Ask people to prepare something in advance
- Encourage people to:

  - listen with full attention
  - express objections and criticism positively
  - act as if the group is powerful — not powerless
  - summarise the previous person's point before making their own
  - rephrase an issue in their own words

- Fix another meeting for items that are cut short
- Choose someone to summarise progress regularly
- Ask for each person's views, letting no one off the hook
- Check everyone leaving knows what to do — ask in a spirit of enquiry, not as a progress chaser

Advice points

MODELLING GOOD BEHAVIOUR

Even when you choose not to chair the meeting, as leader you are clearly a strong focus for attention. People will watch how you are behaving, even when you are saying nothing, or another team member is speaking. If during team meetings you doodle, stare out of the window, slouch in your chair, you are signalling disinterest. People soon notice. Use your body and eyes to encourage people to take part. Nod, smile and stay silent when people talk. Give them your full attention.

Use your voice to convey interest. If you say, in a bored monotone, for instance 'John, that's a great idea,' this merely confirms that you are not valuing their contribution.

ENERGY IS MOVEMENT

It may seem tidy to have everyone sitting in their chairs, dutifully reading their agenda and handling paperwork. Yet this can cause lethargy and loss of attention. Encouraging people to leave their chairs occasionally and move around usually raises energy levels and changes the dynamics of the meeting.

Try asking someone to come to the flipchart and address the meeting, instead of staying in their seat. Consider moving your regular meeting to an unusual venue — even the act of getting there can be a useful energy raiser.

Experiment with using flipchart paper to record people's ideas, posting sheets around the room during the meeting. It makes the meeting more active and reminds people of progress. It also deters repetition. Record decisions in large, legible printing and bring the material to the next meeting if this will help.

When people feel a meeting is wasting time, or they are disinterested in what is happening, they often channel their spare energy into unproductive activity. Doodling, shuffling papers, inventing interruptions or even making elaborate drawings, all reveal that the meeting is not holding people's attention.

You can learn a great deal about your meetings simply by having a look at what people have drawn. Often you see highly artistic scribbling. You do not need to be a psychologist to read anything into these, beyond the raw fact that they have diverted considerable energy away from the meeting.

66 Life energises life. Energy creates energy. It is by spending oneself that one becomes rich. 99
(Sarah Bernhardt)

AGENDAS

Always ensure that there is an agenda, and that everyone can understand it. People want to know what the meeting is about, beyond the bare topic title. They also require time to think about issues. Whenever possible circulate in advance an explanatory agenda or set of aims. If necessary devise one when people arrive and place it in a prominent place.

The person controlling the agenda partly controls the meeting. If you delegate its creation, always review it before circulation. Think of the agenda as a list of things to be done. This is different from a series of items for discussion. Be wary of anything marked only 'for discussion', when you will seldom know what to expect, or what should be the outcome.

The layout and style of agendas can vary considerably, from numbered items and columns to a more free-flowing form of presentation. What matters is giving people essential information, such as whether the item is for decision, exploration, action, or information (see sample agenda).

Packed agendas create pressure and discourage calm discussion. People may leave frustrated, because the meeting has skirted over or missed items. There is a definite art to constructing a team agenda to hold people's interest.

BUILDING AN AGENDA

- State what the item is about
- Indicate how long will it take
- Show who wants it tabled
- Put short, easy items at the beginning
- Place hard items in the middle
- Leave brief information-only items towards the end
- Start and finish with an item involving everyone

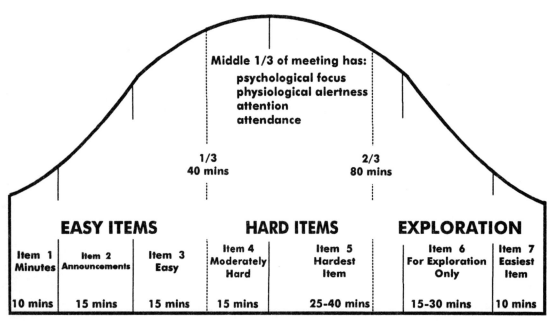

The bell-shaped agenda structure

Agenda
Team meeting: 2.2.95
Time: 2—3.45 pm
Location: Boardroom

TOPIC	TABLED BY	PURPOSE	TIME
Tuning in	All	To 'arrive here'	5
Review of last minutes	Lloyd	Check on action	10
Team outing	Raj	For decision	10
New clients	Leah	Information	5
New computer system	Lloyd	Review needs and a way forward	20
Office move	Leah	Review of options and costs	40
Purchase of new binder	Raj	Information	3
Location of next meeting	Lloyd	For decision	10

Since the whole purpose of a meeting is to have face-to-face communication, it is wasteful to have agenda items more suitable for a smaller meeting, or for sending by memo, fax or E-mail. It may be worth spending time at the start of a meeting checking whether any items can be dealt with differently.

Having the whole team together is expensive. It makes little sense to use the time only to share information, if there is insufficient time for actual decision making. When there is pressure to use the agenda for mainly information items, try having more frequent, shorter meetings.

Some teams meet weekly for half an hour to exchange essential information while still scheduling a formal agenda every two weeks.

MINUTES

Document all formal team meetings. Controlling leaders like to have a secretary take the minutes and issue them later. Supportive leaders write minutes in a way that engages people's interest in the team process.

Poorly led team meetings leave people wondering what is supposed to happen next. Avoid this by adopting action minutes. These reveal only what the meeting decided, rather than describing the discussion. A typical layout for action minutes has as headings:

Topic   Action   By whom   When

There are no reams of descriptive material. Instead the focus is on what will happen next. If non-attenders want more information about what occurred, ask them to contact other team members, rather than expanding the minutes. Attending meetings should be important and missing them ought to be inconvenient.

Even if you delegate the actual job of recording the agreed action, see and approve the minutes before circulation. This ensures that you influence what emerges from team meetings. As you develop trust in the team, you may feel confident enough to do without these checks.

Sticking closely to action minutes makes it so simple to record what happened that it is usually easy to find someone willing to prepare them. If necessary, show how easy it is by temporarily producing them yourself. To speed the production of action minutes, use a flipchart during the team meeting. Ask a member to record the topic, agreed action, by whom and when. After the meeting, remove the flipchart sheet and issue it in typed form.

There are now electronic whiteboards that produce an A4 printout of the written material. These allow immediate photocopying and circulation of the minutes. Simple!

TIME KEEPING

People find meetings satisfying when they start and end on time. To encourage this, always have a clock visible. A novel way of emphasising your passion for timing could be to bring an alarm clock to the meeting. Make it ring to signal the end of the meeting. One team leader used to tell his team, 'This meeting will be one hour long. When that alarm goes, I go. When I go, you go, and the meeting is over.'

Waiting for latecomers merely rewards poor time keeping and prompt arrivals will feel punished if you insist on waiting. Handling late arrivals can be tricky and demands careful diplomacy. You need to be welcoming and make it easy for the person to join in. Yet the nicer you are about someone arriving late, the bigger the 'reward' for disruptive behaviour. Others may conclude that lateness does not really matter.

In offering a welcome to a latecomer, briefly summarise where the meeting has reached and any important decisions. Most people feel bad about arriving late. So unless they are persistent offenders, consider finishing your summary with a phrase such as, 'I hope that fills you in, and we're really glad to see you.'

Tackle persistent late arrivals firmly. Their behaviour disrupts meetings and is a form of leadership challenge. Rather than scolding them in public, discuss privately the reasons for their persistent lateness. It is a mistake to assume that someone is always deliberately late, or disorganised.

If you attach great importance to promptness, show this through always being on time yourself. Some well-known business leaders throw such a tantrum when anyone arrives late that absolutely everyone arrives on time.

By always starting promptly, people soon take good time keeping for granted. Working to time should be a basic rule for how your team operates. Get this established in the early days — it is harder to introduce it later.

Keeping a constant eye on the clock is distracting if you are also chairing the meeting. Consider asking a team member to announce when there are only a few minutes left before an item's deadline. They do the same a few minutes before the meeting is due to end. Try giving this job to someone who regularly arrives late.

People really appreciate a well-run meeting. It values their own time, and allows them to make the best use of it. By insisting on deadlines for your team meetings, people will respect your leadership and be more willing to contribute. If you want to hold really short meetings, use a room without chairs. People will complete the business remarkably quickly! Develop a reputation for meetings that run to schedule.

STAYING ON TRACK

Discussions have a habit of wandering down blind alleys. While your job when chairing a meeting is to prevent this, everyone is responsible for staying focused. Try adopting a team signal to warn about drift. For example, whenever anyone feels the discussion is going astray, they might pointedly wave a hand in a circular motion.

INTERRUPTIONS

Interruptions are such meeting killers that you need a definite strategy to deal with them. Learn to anticipate and handle both external and internal ones. Your best ally in dealing with them is the team itself. If you are firm in your approach most people will support you.

FOUR INTERRUPTION KILLERS

- Act immediately
- Stay calm and friendly
- Be willing to stop or end the meeting immediately
- Invite the team's support to deal with the problem

When dealing with an interruption, consider asking the meeting if everyone agrees with what you are doing. You can usually expect support for your action, giving you strength to deal with any further interruptions.

Breaking off to make phone calls.   Neutralise nearby phones. If someone says they must make a call, ask why, and if it can wait. Tackle this disruptive behaviour immediately.

Shuffling papers noisily.   Be direct. Ask people to handle papers quietly. Try sending a silent signal — for example, catch their eye, press a forefinger to your lips while pointing to your own papers.

Talking during someone's presentation.   Pointedly ask interruptors if they are discussing anything of interest to everyone else, or point out, 'There appear to be two separate meetings going on right now.'

Using a pocket or laptop computer.   Ask the team to confirm that this is not acceptable (which obviously does not apply to someone doing work at the request of the meeting). While the interruptor is fiddling with their keyboard, you might say, 'I think right now everyone should give [the speaker] our full attention.'

Wandering around the room.   Distinguish between *energisers* and *moochers*. Wandering helps energisers be more creative. Thinking aloud and using their physical energy constructively, they stay in touch with the meeting — tolerate them. Moochers want to leave but can't, so look out of windows, pick up objects, and wander about aimlessly — ask them to sit down.

Diversions from the subject under discussion.   Some people are experts at introducing red herrings. Try asking the whole meeting about the diversion — often other people will also say they feel the point is a distraction.

Mobile phones and pagers.   Ask people to switch them off or not to bring them. One team leader turns this into a joke by posting a simulated wild west notice on the door reading *All guns must be left with the sheriff*, crossing out the word 'guns' and inserting 'mobile phones'. If necessary, take the phones in the room off the hook.

Delivered messages and unexpected visitors.   Post a notice on the outside of the door asking unplanned visitors to return later. State where to divert messages, unless they are critical.

Fire drills and noise from building work.   Though it is not entirely predictable, some simple research should reveal if such noise is likely during an important team meeting.

Refreshments.   Organise for these to be already in the room or to arrive at a specified time.

MEETINGS THAT INSPIRE

One important purpose of meetings is to develop the team and its relationships. An important contribution you can make as the leader is to lift team meetings beyond mere efficiency to another level. You aim to make them energising, uplifting, inspiring.

The whole point of a team is the ability to create something together that cannot be achieved by people on their own. So you need to be constantly exploring ways to energise and tap the power inherent in a team. Team meetings are an important place to do this.

Your vital role is to encourage the transformation of meetings into highly rewarding experiences for everyone. This means making time for issues and discussion that transcend the 'day to day'.

For example, ask people to share current concerns, ideas about the future, and their own vision of what should happen. Or ask people to spend a while talking about the team's current values. Are these being lived out in day-to-day work, and if not, why not?

Check how people are feeling. Ask each person to summarise how they feel right now, using one word, or even to make a simple drawing expressing it. Some team leaders always start meetings with a 'safety valve' in which team members briefly share any matter they are feeling strongly about.

Go further and occasionally ask people to bring to the meeting an object that inspires or excites them. It might be a poem, a picture, an object, a story, a piece of music and so on. Sharing these builds links and usually adds a fresh perspective to team relationships.

Convene your team meeting in an inspiring location sometimes. This might be anything from a famous football stadium to a fine art gallery. Meeting in a new place draws attention to the importance of keeping the team alive and stimulated. There may be something to be learned from the local site you are visiting that can be applied to your own organisation.

Try inviting someone unusual from outside the team to address a meeting. For instance, they might talk on a current theme of concern to the team, making their contribution brief yet challenging. Look for what might excite and enthuse your team. They probably have as many good ideas as you on this subject.

INSPIRED TEAM LEADERS PROMOTE

- Communication between all team members
- A forum for participation
- Joint problem solving
- Sharing of ideas
- Creativity and initiative

In their teams everyone has *some* responsibility for:

- Structure
- Methods
- Focusing energy
- Releasing creativity

MONITORING

Make an occasional systematic check on how team meetings are working. Look particularly at:

- *Objectives of the meeting.* Was the team really clear about the purpose?
- *Relevance.* Was the team discussion closely related to the issue?
- *Use of time.* Was the time used efficiently?
- *Participation.* How were contributions handled by the team?
- *Tolerance.* Was tolerance shown of each other's views?
- *Frankness.* How honest was the team with each other?
- *Commitment.* What degree of commitment existed?

ACTION POINTS

 Appoint someone to chair the meeting

 Seek regular comments on what people think of team meetings

 Encourage sharing of ideas on how to make team meetings enlivening

 Encourage regular team meetings

 Ensure everyone is clear about the purpose

 Regularly review goals and processes

 Use regular meetings for important choices, planning and problem solving

 Develop effective ways to encourage people to participate

☑ Model good behaviour in team meetings

☑ Circulate the team agenda or aims for the meeting in advance

☑ Always review the agenda before its circulation

☑ Clarify whether items are for decision, exploration, action, or information

☑ Document all formal team meetings

☑ Use action minutes and issue them promptly

☑ See and approve the minutes before circulation

☑ Have a clock clearly visible during team meetings

☑ Be on time yourself

☑ Develop a reputation for meetings that start and finish on time

☑ Deal with internal and external interruptions

☑ Look for ways to make the meetings inspiring

3 *How to Give Inspired Team Briefings*

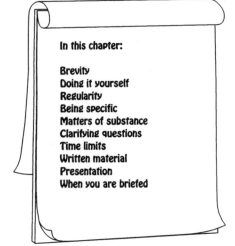

In this chapter:

Brevity
Doing it yourself
Regularity
Being specific
Matters of substance
Clarifying questions
Time limits
Written material
Presentation
When you are briefed

The cops are all there, lounging in their seats. The 'Cap' is up front calling the shots for the day. Another episode of *Hill Street Blues* is under way. Or it could be the lawyers in *LA Law*. On either side of the Atlantic, daily or weekly team briefings are now familiar TV events. Team briefings occur in real life too and have a long history.

The Romans relied on them for ensuring that their generals could indirectly address every centurion. It took hours rather than days for information to get through to the front line.

Team briefings were originally a way of cascading information downwards. These days, with flatter hierarchies and a less military style of leadership, they

TEAM BRIEFINGS

- Promote cooperation
- Help shape individuals into a team
- Strengthen standard setting
- Improve commitment
- Enhance the leadership role
- Counteract the grapevine
- Reduce misunderstandings
- Are for sharing:
    - progress & performance
    - policy and plans
    - people issues
    - points for action

are also powerful tools for upward communication.

A team briefing is concerned with anything sufficiently important to justify bringing everyone together. Be known as a leader willing to share the bad news with the team, just as much as the good news.

Avoid making your team briefings a disciplinary session. Develop your own ways of conveying negative information constructively. For example, if the team fails to achieve a target, focus on improving performance rather than finding someone to blame.

Why do people leave some briefings feeling inspired, while they are only too glad to escape others? Sometimes, of course, it is the subject of the briefing itself. There is nothing particularly uplifting, for instance, in learning about redundancies.

How you convey information is almost as important as the actual content. Most team briefings are a valuable opportunity to inspire and build your team further. They are a chance to share again your positive vision of the future. Treat briefings as a natural extension of regular team meetings.

People will leave the briefing feeling positive, valued and energised if you treat the event with respect. When people see you have carefully prepared, or that you are allowing plenty of time for questions, they are likely to respond positively.

BREVITY

Keep briefings short. Ones that drift on for several hours seldom achieve impact. With bad news, a prolonged briefing easily degenerates into disharmony and bad feeling.

Most briefings can be completed in under an hour. Where the team uses briefings on a daily basis, probably half an hour or 20 minutes will prove sufficient. However, for important issues it is essential not to rush.

IN PERSON

Are you a performer? Briefings place you centre stage, where people expect you to shine. For inspired briefings, you will need to hone your communication skills. The team wants you to do it well, so justify their confidence by preparing carefully.

BRIEFINGS ARE ABOUT COMMUNICATING

Malcolm, a senior manager in a Lloyds firm of underwriters, needed help to improve his ability to handle team briefings. His boss felt he lectured people, even wagging his finger at them when he spoke.

He looked so learned and intelligent, he put off his listeners. They found his unconscious, nervous habit of rocking back and forth on his heels highly distracting. His boss summed up the problem as, 'Malcolm is boringly earnest.'

A specialist in coaching senior managers worked with Malcolm over several one-to-one sessions to improve his briefing skills.

Malcolm disarmingly confessed that many people considered him a tedious briefer. That was rather how he felt about himself. In his anxiety to establish trust, he tended to rely on dispensing large amounts of information.

The specialist coach helped Malcolm improve his flat style of delivery. This required him to be more physical, using his body and hands expressively. Malcolm learned how to use gestures and other body language to support his points.

The help with briefings enabled him to become more relaxed, and draw on his powerful analytical skills for selecting the right information.

You can make the briefing a satisfying experience by keeping it a two-way affair. At its centre is a human being making contact with others. So listening, not just speaking, is essential. Having something special to tell people justifies calling a full team meeting. You can seldom underestimate the team's hunger for well-presented information. You already have far more knowledge than you realise.

Talking point

NEW LISTENINGS

Team briefings are spearheading a new trend in listening by Britain's employers. The Industrial Society conducted a survey among 1000 managers in 1994. They rated team briefings as the best method of communicating with their workforce and hearing staff views. Asked to nominate the most effective way of communicating with employees, over half (57 per cent) of the managers nominated team briefings. The next most effective channel, large staff meetings or 'road shows', scored only 11 per cent. The briefing rated as the best way of getting opinions from employees.

REGULARITY

A football team in the premier league which met once a season to discuss the opposition would not stay at the top for long. Successful football managers insist on weekly team briefings, reviewing opponents' strengths and weaknesses, sharing information, discussing strategy and tactics. They also hold debriefings after matches to analyse how to improve next time.

Briefings build the team through keeping everyone informed. It is tempting to hold them only when there is something big to announce, such as a crisis. They need to be regular rather than sporadic. Even when there is no big announcement to share, bringing the team together is healthy. Reserve regular diary dates for briefings.

Firm dates also help team members plan their time around these occasions. Most can be incorporated into normal team meetings. However, occasionally it may be sensible to set aside a separate time for briefing. This allows communication to be fuller, with less pressure.

Regular is not necessarily frequent. For example, you can hold a formal briefing regularly, twice a year. In practice briefings need to occur sufficiently often for everyone to stay in touch with events. For some teams the right frequency is weekly or even daily. For others, it might be monthly. The nature of the task and the team dictate the timing.

TEAM BRIEFINGS IN FEDERAL EXPRESS

Team briefings are one of Federal Express's main channels for employee communication. Their objective is to promote a good two-way flow of information.

Around 150 work group leaders are the hub of the company's centralised briefing system. Briefings occur monthly, and attendance is monitored. To support the leaders, a core brief is produced by a human resources specialist.

The company's in-house guide explains that a team briefing is:

- a half-hour meeting
- allowing two-way communication
- held monthly and lasting about 30 minutes in company time
- with dates ahead displayed
- led by the work group leader
- monitored by his or her manager

The objectives are to inform employees and to encourage their feedback and total involvement in a process of continuous improvement within their work area.

The content of briefings is:

- core brief
- contract information
- work group information
- performance measures

The first three represent 70 per cent of the time.

BE SPECIFIC

A cardinal briefing principle is to have something worthwhile to say. It needs to be specific and to the point. Team members expect useful information and quickly discern when you are feeding them generalities.

People only absorb a small amount of information when it involves emotional issues, such as ones affecting their jobs or pay. How you convey such information decides whether people will really 'hear' what you say. They usually absorb information best through first seeing the big picture and later understanding the details. However, if the issue affects their immediate lives or jobs, spend only a brief time on the big picture before sharing the personal implications.

TO THE POINT

- Be specific, rather than general
- Explain the precise purpose of the briefing
- Start with a short overview of the whole message
- Break information down, so people receive the most important facts first
- Reduce the message to no more than seven points
- For each point, explain its importance to
  - the team
  - the individual team member
  - you the leader
  - the organisation
  - other parties
- Say what will happen next

SUBSTANCE

Most busy teams receive far too much information. So be sure briefings do not make this worse. Use them only for important matters involving everyone. They are helpful when they extend current knowledge, awareness or understanding. If people attend a few times and find the experience unrewarding, you will find it hard to ensure a full house in the future.

Ensure everyone attends regular briefings, despite other commitments. Make it normal practice to alter diaries to enable attendance. When you cannot convene the whole team, rearrange the meeting or organise for missing members to receive their own briefing session.

You may have new, highly sensitive matters to convey that need handling with care. 'How much should I tell them?' depends partly on how much you trust your team. An essential principle, however, is to assume that *information from all team briefings leaks*. Your own team may be totally discreet about handling sensitive information. Yet it is unwise to assume that secrecy can last long. For instance, other people realise something is afoot when team members suddenly cancel prior engagements at short notice to attend a briefing.

They also guess something important is occurring when people returning from briefings look glum or emotionally affected. For these reasons it is sensible to make team briefings the norm, rather than the exception. Hints and rumours soon replace facts. In deciding how much to tell your team, be guided by what would happen if the information became immediately public.

QUESTIONS

Briefings need to be two-way, not a monologue. Leave time for people to ask questions and discuss the new information. Take seriously the request, 'Has anyone got any questions?' Silence at this point usually only means people are not yet ready to respond. They are probably still absorbing the information and unsure what to ask.

What people tend to ask themselves during a briefing

Advice points

ENCOURAGING PEOPLE TO ENGAGE
● Call a break after the formal briefing
● Suggest people discuss the issue among themselves, in pairs or small groups
● Ask the pairs or groups for their combined comments, concerns, questions
● Deal thoroughly with any issues raised
● If you do not know an answer say so — confirm you will find it out and circulate the new information
● Consider making time for a further meeting and in-depth discussion

TIME LIMITS

Say at the start how long the briefing will take. Follow the timetable to enable people to plan their attendance, even when it is at short notice. A useful device is to request that people arrive early. For example: 'Time: 8.45 am for 9.00 am start.'

This shows you intend to start promptly. Or tell people to come 15 minutes early to socialise and exchange news, before starting the actual briefing.

Where the briefing deals with something unpleasant, your own anxiety may push you to deliver it quickly, leaving immediately afterwards. This will only create trouble later. You need a balance between brevity and an open-ended discussion. A briefing on highly contentious matters can quickly escalate into a difficult situation if there is no clear deadline.

WRITTEN MATERIAL

Briefings are for face-to-face communication, not paperwork. People want to hear from you, or whoever is conducting the session. However, some people absorb information better by sight than sound. Summarise notes on a single sheet for people to take away.

If the issue is too sensitive to be committed to paper, at least write the main points on a flipchart or whiteboard. Remove it at the end of the session.

Document the questions your team raise. You may need to refer these elsewhere for answers. Also when people see you carefully noting questions, they will feel more assured you will eventually answer them. Provide a follow-up mechanism to deal with unfinished matters.

PRESENT WELL

Since briefings are expensive on time, they always need to make an impact. In that sense they are like any other important presentation. Powerful presentations hold people's interest. Even if you are used to speaking to your team, you may still need to develop your abilities. A good presentation can improve your impact and raise your confidence.

BRIEFING STRUCTURE

- Tell them what you are going to tell them
- Tell them
- Tell them what you have just told them

For really important team briefings, spend timing preparing them well and practise your delivery. Good presenters rehearse hard and often.

You need a definite purpose for talking to the team. For example, do you want to interest, enthuse, get action, promote discussion or what? If you could just as easily achieve what you want through writing it down, a verbal encounter is wasteful.

Establishing a 'presence' is not a mysterious talent only possessed by great leaders. You have it when you are present, awake and alive in the room, giving your full attention to your team. It is being totally sensitive to what is happening around you. It allows you to realise when your briefing is going well, and when it is not. Because you are completely alert to what your audience needs, they will give you their full attention.

Before starting your briefing:

- Stop
- Look
- Breathe
- Listen

You *stop* before you start! That is, when you are poised to begin your briefing, do not rush into it the moment you are centre stage. Instead, pause to allow your audience to become used to you in the limelight. Give everyone time to settle down. This pause might last five seconds or longer.

Look around and take in the room. With a dozen people, there is time to give eye contact to everyone before you begin — acknowledging their existence, perhaps smiling at some people.

Experienced actors suffers nerves talking to a group of people. Why should you be immune? Before speaking give yourself time to take several steady breaths. This lets the oxygen reach your brain and allows the calming effects to work.

Listen carefully to the sounds around you. Is there a shuffling of papers, are people still fidgeting or appearing unsettled? Wait until you achieve the silence and attention which your presence and the important briefing deserve.

ESSENTIALS OF A POWERFUL PRESENTATION

- *Preparation* — the material, anticipating audience needs, organising presentation aids, rehearsal
- *Purpose* — knowing what you want to achieve
- *Presence* — being fully 'there'
- *Passion* — putting commitment into it
- *Personality* — using your unique assets

You can find out more about improving your presentations by reading our book *Perfect Presentations* (Century Business).

WHEN YOU ARE BRIEFED

A briefing often stems from one you first receive from someone else. You need to convey to your team both the information, and the sentiments and flavour of what you heard.

Suppose you receive an enthusiastic presentation about your company's new policy of changing to mainly part-time staff. You will need to convey to your team both the facts and the enthusiasm for the new policy.

If you ask someone to brief an absent member, ensure this person really understands the issues at stake. They must convey both facts and the more intangible sentiments and flavour which underpinned the original briefing.

ATTENDING A BRIEFING

- Keep notes on what you hear — stick to the main points
- Ask questions on behalf of your team
- Clarify what may be shared with your team

Give team briefings in person

 Offer regular briefings

 Be specific

 Make time for questions

 Provide written material where possible

 Present briefings well

 Keep to a definite time limit

 Cover what people need to know, the implications, and what will happen next

 Use well-tried methods for ensuring a good briefing delivery: Preparation, Purpose, Presence, Passion, Personality

When attending briefings on your team's behalf keep notes on what you hear, ask questions, clarify what can be shared with your team

How to Set Inspiring *4* Team Goals

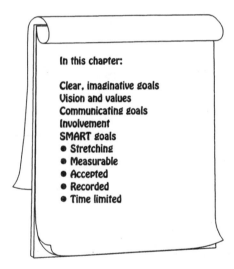

In this chapter:

Clear, imaginative goals
Vision and values
Communicating goals
Involvement
SMART goals
● Stretching
● Measurable
● Accepted
● Recorded
● Time limited

Houston Ground Control of NASA hears this conversation between four astronauts who have just been shot into space:

'Hey guys, we're on our way. Mars, here we come.'
'Captain, you mean the moon.'
'Didn't anyone tell you?'
'Tell us what?'
'This trip we're going to Mars.'
'We are? But I thought we were going to the moon.'
'Houston Ground Control here. Just let's get things straightened out. You're there to repair the Hubble telescope, who said anything about the moon or Mars?'

If this scenario sounds a little crazy, consider a survey by the Cranfield School of Management in the early 1990s. This found that one in three British managers disagreed about their company's future shape and direction. The study stated:

> **"** For a top management team to share a coherent vision of the future, the team needs a high quality dialogue and a shared understanding. **"**

Apparently many directors never have this high quality dialogue, with predictable results. This is not much different from footballers thinking they should score runs or astronauts getting their destination wrong.

For example, nearly two out three senior executives complained there were obstacles to achieving objectives within the senior team. Many were of their own making. A common problem is a lack of clear objectives in the first place.

CLEAR GOALS

Most reasonably competent team leaders realise they are responsible for helping the team establish goals. But they are often puzzled about how to define goals that are sufficiently clear, that tap into people's motivation.

The purpose of clear goals is to ensure that people know what the team is trying to achieve, mobilising their enthusiasm, curiosity, energy, creativity and talent. Goals justify the team's existence.

CLEAR GOALS

The top management team of Braintree Council asked itself in 1983, 'What is the Authority good at?' It went on to establish some core values and a clear corporate goal:

'Braintree Council wishes, as one of its primary objectives, to be regarded as the best authority in England for its citizens, its Members and its staff.'

It later set out what it meant by 'best'. By 1994 it had won a string of public recognition rewards, including nomination as the best local authority in the UK. It went forward to the finals of a worldwide competition involving 1.5 million authorities.

Whether you personally set the goals or rely on the team to establish them matters less than the nature of those goals. Truly inspired goals convert boring statistical statements, often expressed as targets, into more uplifting aims that excite team members, stimulating them to go that extra mile. They capture the imagination and release people's potential.

You nearly always find an imaginative goal underpinning a successful team. Often it is the leader who articulates it, sometimes it evolves from team discussion. The important point is that it exists.

VISION

Sometimes the team itself meets initially to tackle an important new goal. This virtually becomes the team's vision, its *raison d'être*. A team's vision is what it aspires to in the future. It answers the question: 'What do we want to *be*?'

A VISION:

- Remains constant in some essential form
- Incorporates a meaningful goal
- Centres on people

Vision is not the same as the central task facing a team. A task is seldom sufficient to sustain the team over weeks, months and perhaps years of working together. Thus the vision is a long-range picture of the future. A challenging one may never be fully realised, since it really expresses a strategic intent. This differs from the more prosaic yet equally important goals underpinning it.

Team visions stated in inspiring or uplifting ways may be memorable, yet this will not guarantee that they stand the test of time. They still require detailed goals and targets. By themselves, they are merely words. It is the supporting goals and the behaviour of the team that bring the vision to life.

After reviewing what it was there for, the newly formed management team at the Badshot Lea garden centre in Surrey expressed its vision, not its detailed goals, as:

'The seeds of our success grow through our customer commitment, cultivating our staff and weeding out the competition.'

To outsiders the metaphor might seem somewhat forced. To insiders though, it admirably summed up their vision. The garden centre has since become one of the top three earners in the garden centre industry.

Analysis of Lee Iacocca's leadership at Chrysler suggests that much of the power of his strategic initiatives stemmed from his use of metaphors. And Steve Wozniak, the co-founder of Apple Computers, described his fellow founder Steve Jobs as always able to 'couch things in the right words'.

A team vision should excite and inspire people. It often comes as quite a shock to realise that your role is helping the team find what excites and inspires them. Old-style controlling leaders seldom see it that way. They rely mainly on using authority to define what will be done and by whom.

Leaders search for and use people's wish to do something — their inner motivation. This may mean changing unexciting goals set from outside the team into ones that get people's creative juices flowing. Without stimulating goals to set people on fire, leadership is hard to sustain.

The challenge to develop the first 32-bit minicomputer, for instance, proved utterly engrossing for everyone concerned. A secretary on the project led by the visionary leader Tom West who complained about the hard work and excessive hours explained to an outsider why she did not quit. 'Oh I can't leave... I just have to see how it turns out. I just have to see what Tom's going to do next.'

There is much nonsense talked about so-called visionary leaders. The apparently impossible demands seem almost calculated to make you feel inadequate. You could easily conclude that only exceptional people can lead. Being a visionary leader does not imply you are prescient. It means being:

- clear about what you want
- able to ask for help in achieving clarity
- willing to stake your reputation, even career, on achieving the vision

Most people do not come to work excited about increasing the organisation's annual profit, even if they have a financial stake in it. The best visions are those that give people a feeling they are engaged in something truly worthwhile which affects other people.

Thus a global pharmaceutical company inspires its staff with constant reminders that they are not merely striving to produce better drugs. They are at work to improve the health of mankind. The Body Shop's employees are not bothered much about another set of good annual results, they enjoy being part of a company that is committed to making an impact in the community.

Visionary leadership is not a mechanical quality — like a hypodermic needle with the active ingredient of vision injected into the team to inspire. It is much more like a drama in which communication and action occur simultaneously. It is a process of an idea being repeated often, giving it life through words and action. Thus a leader's vision has an immediacy and vitality that ideas like profits or return on capital never acquire for most people.

The visionary leader thus shares many of the characteristics of an actor in representing a picture of the future that inspires. It is, for example, hard to find a visionary leader who is not also good at using language skilfully to stimulate and motivate, through both logic and appeals to emotion.

In essence, visionary leaders create drama, they turn work into play. You want to be part of what they are offering.

- Express the vision
- Behave in ways which advance the goal of making it happen
- Explain the vision so people know what is required in terms of specific action
- Extend the vision, applying it to various situations
- Expand the vision, using it in many different ways, in a wide range of circumstances

Finally, leaders develop a real knack for going beyond the vision to show people exactly how they can contribute to realising it. This is much harder than it sounds. It is all very well visualising your company as a world leader in making jeans, for example — but how do you help the ordinary machinist or van driver understand how they can play a meaningful part in the attainment of such a formidable dream?

In our own company, for instance, we have a strong vision of the kind of development centre we want to create and how we envisage our clients transforming the way they obtain the best from their people. Yet such a dream needs to be turned into a more practical message for an administrator, a project manager or a bookkeeper. This means spending time with them to help them understand how their work directly or indirectly can contribute to the realisation of the dream. For example, one aspect that supports our vision is providing a highly responsive, caring service to our clients.

Thus the job of the administrator is to ensure that all our systems underpin this requirement, from phones being answered rapidly, to sending out brochures quickly in response to new enquiries. Similarly, the bookkeeper can contribute to the vision through ensuring that our invoices are always clear, with the correct amounts shown, and sent out on time.

COMMUNICATING GOALS

It does not follow that because you feel challenged by a goal, others will feel the same. How you express it can be as important as the goal itself, so try to be enthusiastic and confident. Listen to the team's ideas about how to achieve it.

It will certainly also help your team if you explain goals by breaking them down into more detailed activities, with accompanying deadlines.

Talking point

GOALS EMPLOYERS MOST WANT TOP TEAMS TO ACHIEVE	
A survey of 100 directors and senior managers in UK and multinational companies revealed the following preferred goals:	
Deliver customer satisfaction	77%
Achieve total quality	74%
Overcome departmental barriers	65%
Encourage cross-functional cooperation	63%
Change the corporate culture	63%
Involve employees	63%
Increase speed of response	56%
Build closer relationships with customers	55%
Improve managerial productivity	49%
Harness individual talents	48%
Source: Adaptation (*Personnel Today*, 1994)	

Old-style controlling leaders establish goals themselves and simply impose them, often against people's wishes. While this can work, it can also breed resentment and resistance. It is certainly disempowering.

Today, organisations are introducing ever flatter hierarchies, giving more responsibility to those at the front line. Combine these factors with the need to keep improving quality, and you have a powerful case for learning to tap everyone's contribution. In such situations a rigid cascading process of imposed goals seldom works well.

NO CASCADING

To achieve its training objectives, SmithKline Beecham abandoned the hierarchical system. It was simply a failure when senior managers who attended a programme were expected to pass information and skills on to middle managers, who in turn were expected to pass them on to subordinates.

Now the company takes mixed rank working groups, and aims for an immediate impact on the entire team.

It is a matter of leadership style whether goals come down from the top, like tablets from the mountain, or become established as foundation stones from the bottom upwards. Generally though, a straight top-down, cascading effect is harder to sustain.

The benefits of involving people when choosing goals usually outweigh the cost of the extra time taken to enrol them. Once people have 'signed on' willingly, you obtain far more from them than by merely announcing what they must achieve.

If you decide to seek the team's involvement in deciding what needs to be done, you may still be unsure how far to go. It takes time to involve people and they will consequently have certain expectations about the process. They soon realise if there is manipulation, and if you have no intention of making use of their views.

IMPOSED GOALS

Limit debate
Minimise uncertainty
Override conflicts
Useful in a crisis
Simplify communications
Reflect management priorities
Inspire or challenge
Reduce personal autonomy

Saying you believe in participation is not enough. People expect you to prove it by your actions. Be clear about what you mean by consultation and participation. Confusion makes involvement in goal setting more difficult. It is always worth clarifying what is on offer.

- *Consultation* is when you seek an opinion. You are saying: 'I will listen to your views and perhaps consider them in the final decision.'

- *Participation* is where you offer to use their views. You are promising: 'You will have a real say in the final choice.'

Most people readily accept that certain goals are not negotiable. For instance, outside forces such as senior management or legislation may impose them. Where there is no scope for participation it is better to say: 'This is not negotiable, we must do it.'

If you are a smoker trying to give up the habit, experts will advise you to declare your intention to all your friends and work colleagues. Going public with an intention means you feel under pressure to deliver. The same applies to team goals. It places everyone's reputation on the line, providing a considerable incentive to succeed.

Consider pinning the goals up in a prominent place within the team work area, to remind everyone what is at stake.

SMART GOALS

There is often a confusion in teams over vision, goals, objectives and targets, since the meaning of these can differ from one organisation to another. It is sensible if you can agree on a common language, at least within the team.

NEGOTATED GOALS

Encourage creativity
Promote participation
Gain commitment
Develop trust
Encourage responsibility
Expand individual influence
Value people
Promote personal autonomy

VISION, GOALS AND TARGETS

Vision is the grand picture, what the team aspires to.

Example:

- To be the bank everyone considers going to first

Goals describe the steps to achieving the vision.

Example:

- Goal 1   Have more high street branches than any competitor, by the end of the decade
- Goal 2   Offer the fastest counter service in Britain, as measured by industry norms, by the end of the decade
- Goal 3   Give all customers the service they need, plus a bit more — as measured by independent consumer studies, by the end of next year

Goals and objectives mean the same thing.

Targets are the more detailed results for reaching an objective.

Example:

- Goal 1   To have more high street branches than any competitor, by the end of the decade
- Target 1   Identify 700 suitable properties for purchase or lease by year end
- Target 2   Complete purchase on 200 properties by year end
- Target 3   Refurbish at least 20% of all new premises by year end
- Target 4   Open to the public 30+ new branches by year end

Since goals are usually the broad aims of the team, there should normally only be a few, perhaps five or six. When goals describe the direction the team is taking they are strategic and answer the question: 'Where are we heading?'

How can you help your team pick goals people find

really useful? Try using the SMART method in which goals
are: Stretching, Measurable, Accepted, Recorded and
Time limited.

Stretching goals use people's full potential. Because they
encourage people to reach beyond their present limits or
experience, they offer excitement and challenge. They do
not always need to be entirely realistic. This may sound
unworldly, yet a goal is only stretching if there is some
uncertainty about whether it is reachable. Stretching
goals are always risky in some way. Only through reaching
for a risky goal does it later become clear whether it is a
realistic one.

STRETCHING

USE STRETCHING GOALS TO:

- Pose a challenge
- Excite people
- Create controlled risk
- Tap people's creative, inner resources

Often a team faces goals set by outsiders, such as a
senior management group, a demanding customer, or
legislation. These may be initially expressed in
uninteresting ways without posing a challenge or creating
any excitement.

   This is where you use your imagination and tap into
the creative flair of your team. Take the original goal and
reframe it, by expressing it a new or different way. For
example, a simple goal to exceed last year's sales by 20
per cent is hardly exciting. It may sound more appealing
when reframed as: 'Our goal is to smash the 20 per cent
barrier.'

   Or consider the goal adopted by one highly innovative
plastics company. It set a target of producing many new
products, or improvements to existing ones. It then
converted this general aim into the more understandable
one of producing one new product for every day of the
year.

Another way to reframe a goal is to exceed expectations. For example, one retail chain set a specific goal for the delivery of supplies to its shops by a contractor. The goal was expressed as: 90 per cent of all deliveries to be within two hours of the agreed delivery period. The contractors inspired their drivers by asking them to beat this, by aiming for at least 95 per cent.

Reframing can be through deciding to reach goals faster, cheaper, better, in a different way to the original expectation. For example, in Levi Strauss' Blue Ridge jeans factory, production was reorganised around teams of about 35 people. Although the plant management sets minimum goals, the teams set their own targets over and above this minimum.

MEASURABLE

Measurable goals are specific, stating the aim unambiguously. This statement may be part of the goal definition or an added part that comes later. What matters is a numerical statement that allows you to know whether or not the goal has been achieved.

You make an important contribution as a team leader by pushing to make goals measurable. If you regularly do this, you may be pleasantly surprised at how much impact you achieve.

If you cannot measure a goal, how do you know you whether you have reached it? For example, the team leader may say 'We have a long way to go.' The team's response could be, 'We already got there.'

Although at least one famous management guru loves to say, 'If you cannot measure it you cannot manage it', not all goals lend themselves to precise measurement. Some, for example, may need expressing in broad terms, while leaving the measurable part for the more detailed targets.

ACCEPTED

Effective team goals are also accepted. People agree to commit themselves fully to trying to achieve them. Without such agreement, goals are likely to remain aspirations, rather than becoming successful outcomes.

With a controlling style of leadership you simply set the

goals and others dutifully try to achieve them. You do not worry much about whether people go along with the aims. This is a normal way of working in many cultures. In many Western organisations, however, it is proving an increasingly unsuccessful way of achieving outstanding results.

To persuade team members to strive hard for a particular goal, you may need help turning it into one they feel they own. This allows the person to relate what they want, to what the team or the organisation needs. You will therefore have to uncover for each team member: 'What's in it for me?'

For the team to accept a goal they must believe it is both desirable and potentially achievable. Initially people may reject some goals because they appear unrealistic, until force or circumstances, good leadership or new information persuades them otherwise.

A sales manager, for example, may set his or her team the goal of increasing sales by 50 per cent next year. They are likely to reject it if they see it as totally impossible to achieve. Through persuasion and influence the manager must convince them to suspend judgement on whether it is realistic or not.

ACCEPTABLE GOALS

People recognise a goal as acceptable if they believe it might be worth striving for, despite appearing initially to be unrealistic. Motorola asked a team of engineers to create a production line for mobile phones. The senior management stipulated a failure rate of only one in several million. Shocked at first, the team felt the aim was desirable, although apparently unrealistic.

Their creativity and natural desire for a challenge took over. They accepted the objective, adding their own twist of doing it sooner than the management expected. They finished with a couple of weeks to spare.

That experience has stood the company in good stead. Its Total Customer Satisfaction programme has gained worldwide recognition and radically influenced team goals. Motorola's quality programme applies to everything it does. This is a soundly based statistical concept in which the defect rate for any process is no more than 3.4 parts per million opportunities for error. Previously such success seemed utterly impossible.

Teams throughout the company face demands for tenfold continuous improvement in two years. All production processes, for instance, have a goal of tenfold improvement in five years.

Motorola does not simply impose such goals. It carefully researches their feasibility. To help obtain people's acceptance of seemingly impossible targets, it invests one per cent of sales turnover in training and development.

RECORDED

Recorded goals prevent the team losing sight of what it is trying to achieve. You can keep a single goal in your head. It's harder if there are five or six goals. You need a foolproof way of remembering and keeping track of each.

RECORDED GOALS TO SHOW

- What we are aiming to achieve
- Whether we have achieved our aims
- How far we are succeeding (or failing)

Record goals by writing them in a file, notebook, or a secure place. You may find it helpful to keep your team's goals permanently visible, pinning them on flipchart paper in a prominent place.

Recording goals and monitoring progress encourages everyone to stay clear about what is happening. However, excessive detail can produce confusion and reduce interest in progress. List the more detailed information about the complex stages of a major project on separate schedules.

TIME LIMITED

Goals should be time limited. That is, people need to know when they must achieve them. Setting time boundaries not only makes better use of resources, it focuses people's minds on a definite end date.

TIME LIMITS

- Clarify urgency
- Focus team energy
- Communicate goals to non-team members
- Set standards of performance

Goals without time boundaries degenerate into mere wishing. Without a sense of urgency the natural human tendency is to tackle more pressing matters.

Choose time boundaries to which everyone can relate. Deadlines of two or three years are hard to get excited about. They may need to be reduced to more practical, shorter-term steps.

Setting time limits that the team constantly ignores merely undermines confidence and it will be increasingly hard to get the best from the team. Encourage it to adopt the ground rule of never missing deadlines, apart from truly exceptional circumstances.

Time boundaries have to be adapted to reflect changing circumstances. Use evidence about what is happening in the real world, rather than sticking blindly to a set of deadlines. Inevitably, some will need altering in response to new situations.

☑ Good leaders set inspiring, challenging goals

☑ Be clear about what you mean by vision, goals, objectives and targets

☑ Develop a clear and attractive picture of what you want

☑ Communicate what you want, so others want to be part of it

☑ Clarify whether you want consultation or participation when setting goals

☑ Make goals public and share them beyond the team

☑ Show people what must happen to realise the vision

☑ Translate general goals into ones that tap into the team's enthusiasm

☑ Try to be enthusiastic and confident about team goals

☑ Listen to the team's ideas about how to achieve goals

☑ Use SMART goals: Stretching, Measurable, Accepted, Recorded, Time limited

☑ Build the team ground rule of always hitting deadlines

How to Grow 5
Self-Managing Teams

In this chapter:

Growth of self-managing teams
Myths
Job satisfaction
Tasks
Management benefits
Productivity and quality
Stepping out
Learning requirements
The tough bits

Imagine allowing a whole bunch of undisciplined people to decide their own wages. As for permitting them to choose what to do, and when to arrive for work, how absurd can you get? Yet for some companies these freedoms sum up the essence of self-managing teams.

Around half of America's largest companies now claim to have self-managing teams. In Britain most manufacturing concerns (57 per cent) were considering changing the roles of managers and supervisors in 1994. Something strange is happening to the management of teams. Companies such as Brazil's Semco or W L Gore in the US have attracted world attention by breaking apparently inviolate rules of organisational life. Everything from setting wages and production targets to hierarchies and supervision is being challenged. To a traditional, controlling manager, self-managing teams are nonsense.

Rather than 'management', self-managing teams demand empowerment. This much abused word is nothing more than putting people in charge, 'owning' the whole process from start to finish.

Ideas like quality circles have been around for years. They have relied on work teams reaching a rough agreement about what needs to be done to improve the team's output. So how different is a self-managing team, and do you really want one?

Broadly it is a small work group of around 5 to 15 people who share responsibility for a particular task. They have skills and authority to supervise themselves daily, reaching decisions previously made by someone placed in formal authority over them. For example, such teams can usually decide who does what within the team and how to solve a particular problem when it crops up.

In this kind of team, everyone tends to learn all the tasks that need to be done. So in that sense it is entirely different to the traditional situation where jobs are broken down into ever smaller components, in each of which someone specialises.

The whole process is a gradual one, as teams become learning centres, constantly discovering how to take more responsibility. For instance, the team may eventually become responsible for ordering the materials or information that they require. In such teams leadership changes from telling to helping.

THE WL GORE EXPERIENCE

W L Gore is a world leader in breathable rainwear fabric and cable insulation, with a turnover of $1 billion. It was one of the first companies to abandon the traditional hierarchy in favour of a horizontal organisation. Its 5000 associates, not employees, work in an environment with:

- no fixed or assigned authority
- no job titles
- no one is hired until an associate sponsors them on a trial basis
- person-to-person communication
- objectives set by those who must make them happen
- no budgets
- work organised through processes and commitment

The goal is to make money and have fun.

To some managers, a self-managing team is a wonderful way to abandon any responsibility for results, since you no longer have any power to say 'get on with it.' Uncomfortable jobs like appraisal, discipline and setting targets now belong elsewhere. It is not surprising that the drive for self-managing teams often comes not from personnel experts but from senior divisional or plant line managers.

It is a common myth of self-managing teams that they will do all the previously nasty bits of managing. Those in charge naturally believe they themselves will be left with the more uplifting roles such as communication, making big decisions, dealing with even more senior management. Self-managing teams still need managing though, often in new and challenging ways.

THE SEMCO EXPERIENCE

The ultimate example of the self-managing team in action is the Brazilian company Semco. In his entertaining book *Maverick!* (Arrow, 1993), owner Ricardo Semler describes how he gradually turned a highly controlling company into a fully self-managing one.

There are no managers or leaders in the conventional sense. The old-style pyramid structure has gone, replaced by just three concentric circles of organisation. The smallest, inner circle is a team of half a dozen people coordinating general policies and strategies. The second circle encloses seven to ten leaders of Semco's business units, called partners. Everyone else is an associate and is in the largest, outer circle. In this largest circle there are triangles to represent a single person, called a coordinator.

Coordinators are the first crucial level of management — the marketing, sales, production advisers. It is more than mere symbolism. Where there were once bosses, supervisors and departmental heads, now there are a few coordinators. A coordinator cannot report to another coordinator, and an associate cannot report to another associate.

This radical shift has attracted attention from all over the world. The absence of structure amazes visitors. As Semler himself explains: 'even the most cynical observers were astonished to find that things were better off once we got rid of the pyramid and all its rungs and roles.'

The company has prospered financially and, as if determined to continue amazing people, now permits certain individuals and teams to set their own salaries.

MYTHS ABOUT SELF-MANAGING TEAMS

- *They don't need managers.* False: they still need managing, through coaching, facilitation and support.
- *They don't need leaders.* False: leadership is essential and is often shared right across the team.
- *They make leaders powerless.* False: leaders must exercise power differently, through using influence.
- *They happen automatically.* False: it takes time for newly created teams to evolve; team members may need intensive training; some people never want to work that way.
- *They only succeed in certain industries.* False: they have worked well in everything from manufacturing to insurance, from telecommunications to banking.
- *They are cheap.* False: in the short term they may cost more than traditional methods, with high setting-up overheads such as training, redeployment and troubleshooting.
- *They are quickly established.* False: companies like Procter and Gamble have spent decades working to get the self-managing idea to work for them.

SELF-MANAGING TEAMS IN PRACTICE

Laura Ashley

The Laura Ashley design group required a special effort to help its managers adapt to self-managing teams and become leaders. They needed to switch from using power to relying mainly on influence. As an internal human resource adviser put it: 'They had to have faith, to learn to let go, while still taking some responsibility.'

Remuneration rewarded only individual effort and therefore undermined rather than reinforced team working. The company eventually made up to 4 per cent of the total salary bill available for specialist pay for encouraging the self-managing process.

Body Shop

Following a number of experiments in the Body Shop, the concept was extended to a number of stores and even to the human resource department itself. However, the company found that self-managing teams tended to work best when staff were recruited from scratch.

Kimberley-Clark

The Body Shop experience was mirrored at Kimberley-Clark. It too learned that the best results came from entirely new teams. Members were recruited through personality tests and the company selected only those people thought to be most suitable for a team working environment.

LandRover

Watch a team on the production line at LandRover and you will be hard pressed to decide who exactly is in charge. Yet someone is apparently filling in those coloured charts, showing who has what skills, or who has still some way to go before they can do all the jobs. People are clearly making decisions, ranging from whether to stop the production line to offering help to a colleague.

Dettmers Industry

This Florida-based company makes seating for aircraft and employs around 30 people. Teams of five or six machinists and welders were given the freedom to determine their own pay and even decide whether to employ more staff. Productivity rose by 60 per cent.

You could be interested in growing a self-managing team for several highly practical reasons, starting with more job satisfaction. Although you cannot order people around, in exchange you obtain greater commitment and involvement. Another reason is you can stop being the only one to worry about certain issues. These might include who operates what machine, what hours people will work, when to take breaks, which work is defective, and how to stick within budget.

You no longer have to be the only one resolving problems with suppliers, customers or important internal departments. Anyone in the team might decide such a contact is necessary and initiate it themselves.

If you grow a self-managing team you also stop being the only person who agonises over targets, performance appraisals or even who to fire. These are now all shared between you and the team. In some sense, you can even stop worrying about being the formal leader. Everyone may lead from time to time.

SELF-MANAGING TASKS	
Prepare budgets	Select new members
Control quality	Resolve conflicts
Keep records	Monitor performance
Solve problems	Control stock
Make decisions	Control absences and lateness
Maintain discipline	Plan goals
Induct new members	Provide leadership
Assign work	Seek information

Advice points

What is so special about self-managing teams that many organisations are rushing headlong into them? The two main reasons are productivity and quality. Where self managed teams have succeeded they have produced large increases in productivity, sharp drops in the time it takes to complete tasks, and massive improvement in quality. All this with usually many fewer people.

Support functions such as administration, previously only tenuously connected with the team, are now integrated, becoming more meaningful. Often these functions are no longer performed by functional specialists, they are shared by everyone. Instead of taking administration for granted, regarding it as a chore or irrelevant, now it is an intrinsic part of how the team operates. Everyone, for example, wants to make sure information about quality, or skills, is available.

LEVI'S LEADERSHIP

Levi Strauss goes for self-managing teams in a big way after their huge success in key US factories. Teams now make complete garments, rather than doing only part of the production, such as sewing on pockets. The teams hire their own people and are responsible for their own work hours and scheduling. Direction is from the ranks, not above. Everyone is given extensive training in team skills and leadership.

The results include a one-third reduction in 'seconds', the time between order and shipment has fallen by 10 days, and a pair of jeans is now made in one day, not five.

STEPPING OUT

If you decide a self-managing team is for you, how do you go about creating it? You will almost certainly need the commitment of your own boss, if you have one. Because of the time it takes to grow such a team, you also need plenty of understanding and tolerance while you get it right.

Be sure you know why you are taking this step. There need to be sound business reasons. These could include productivity, better quality, greater customer satisfaction, lower staff turnover, and so on. It is not enough to choose the self-managing team option merely because someone else is doing it.

Once you have decided that a self-managing team could produce outstanding results for you, share this conclusion with those who must set up the teams or who will be in one. Just about everyone in contact with the team needs to be alerted to what is happening. Tell everyone, not just managers, trainers or team members.

If you have several teams reporting to you, try initiating the self-managing idea with only one, before going wider. Learn from your mistakes, using the knowledge to guide any further expansion. A step-by-step method is usually preferable. When you have chosen a team to become self-managing, you need to take a long-term view. It will not happen instantly. People need time to grow and develop, to understand that the approach is here to stay.

Standing in front of a house plant and shouting 'grow, damn you, grow' is likely to be less effective than watering it. Likewise, in growing self-managed teams you cannot exhort people to make them work. You rely on their natural wish to cooperate and develop themselves as people. While some will welcome the idea, others will take time to get used to it. Expect some resistance. Be concerned if you cannot detect resistance somewhere in the team: this could mean people do not yet fully understand what is involved.

Resistance does not mean you cannot proceed. It does mean you have to try to anticipate reasons for resistance, and be ready to deal understandingly with people's fears and feelings. Adopt positive actions, such as making sure you fully explain what will happen. Keep communicating throughout the change. Be sure also that there is proper training for those involved.

SELF-MANAGED TEAMS — PEOPLE MAY NEED TO LEARN:

- How to brainstorm
- That they can be creative, imaginative and inventive
- How to solve different sorts of problems
- Specific statistical tools
- Methods of dealing with conflict
- About the nature of leadership
- Ways to measure what they are doing
- Different ways to talk to each other
- The limits of their own authority
- To trust their own judgement

A consequence of growing a self-managing team is the need to review remuneration. Such teams rely on people cooperating rather than competing. Even when there is friendly rivalry about who can produce the best results, it is in the context of overall team performance. So in self-managing teams, for example, it is much harder to claim personal credit for success. Everyone contributes to the result and you may never know quite who has really made the final difference. Pay therefore needs to reflect a mixture of individual and team rewards.

Talking point

'WE DID IT', NOT 'I DID IT'

In our own company we once sat talking about a new customer. After prolonged contact but no purchase she finally hired our services. One member of our team claimed this buying decision was because they had recently met the customer at a conference and reminded her about our services.

Another person mentioned spending time recently on the phone giving the customer lots of detailed information. Yet another person declared they had taken the customer out to lunch a few months back. We needed to remind ourselves that our success was a team effort. We had all 'done it'.

THE TOUGH BITS

Growing a self-managing team can be a rocky road to travel. Some boulders you encounter may be entirely unexpected, for example the strong wish by some people for continued supervision. An important loss they may feel is not having someone in charge who sorts out disagreements within the team. It can take some time for people to get used to making their own decisions.

In self-managing teams, conflicts and disputes can easily escalate, because the leader no longer has total authority. Instead of pushing disagreements under the carpet, self-managing teams usually bring them out for resolution. This is a healthy tendency. So if you are promoting a self-managing team, you need to explore ways to handle conflict, without resorting to traditional controlling behaviour. For example, you can help the team learn how to value its differences.

IT MAY NOT WORK FIRST TIME

The Eaton Corporation's Manchester-based truck component division's first attempt to introduce self-managing teams 'failed miserably', according to Alan Best, its European senior executive.

'The main problem was that people we were trying to get to act in a self-managed way weren't ready for it. They didn't understand what they had to do, or how to cope. We did have training but it was not long enough, deep enough or continual enough. After about six months people came back and said, "We don't like this, we need somebody to talk to us, to supervise us, to schedule our work, to look after our salaries." As an organisation we were totally unready for it.'

Eventually the company got it right, through its approach to total quality management.

Another boulder you may stumble on is your own lack of knowledge. The nature of the self-managing team is such that people know far more about the team, and the organisation as a whole, than you do. Because they have taken responsibility they want far more information about anything that might impinge on their own sphere of influence. With such informed people it is no longer easy to treat them as 'mere employees'. They are much more like partners in the whole enterprise and expect appropriate treatment.

Almost by definition, self-managing teams are close, people build strong relationships with each other, there are high levels of mutual trust. This makes it hard for someone new to join. A new member can often radically alter the entire dynamic of the team. A bad recruitment decision can therefore severely upset the team and cause enormous resentment. If you previously held the sole right of appointment, you will almost certainly have to relinquish it.

Self-managing teams usually choose their own candidates, rather than have new members imposed on them. This means the whole team may want to vet any possible new members and this can take quite a time. Still, it will almost certainly be worth it. Teams are often better at making recruitment choices than individuals, especially when they have a big investment in the result.

66 Managers have also had to struggle with the critical balance between control and abdication and, in some cases when they have the balance right, their new, less directive style has come as a shock to people used to being told what to do and when to do it. Suddenly provided with the power of decision-making they have felt bewildered, unsupported and 'dumped-on'. Coaching workshops are being run to address these issues. 99
(Kevin Gleeson,
leadership trainer in the 32,000-employee retail company
W H Smith)

ACTION POINTS

 Beware of the myths about self-managing teams

 Responsibility for a variety of previous managerial or supervisory functions is shared by the whole team

 Self-managing teams offer a powerful way of increasing both productivity and quality

 You will need the commitment and understanding of your own boss to introduce a self-managing team

✔ There must be sound business reasons for growing a self-managing team, such as productivity, better quality, greater customer satisfaction, lower staff turnover, and so on

✔ Share widely the decision to grow a self-managing team as quickly as possible

✔ Introduce self-managing teams slowly and learn from your mistakes

✔ Take a long-term view: such teams do not happen instantly

✔ Expect some resistance: its absence could mean people do not yet realise what is involved

✔ Anticipate resistance and plan how to deal with it

✔ People may require a new set of skills before they can successfully work in a self-managing team

✔ Pay may need to reflect a mixture of individual and team rewards

✔ People may miss being supervised because this suppressed conflicts

✔ Learn how to handle conflict without resorting to traditional managerial controlling behaviour

✔ Changing team members can cause particular problems

✔ Self-managing teams usually choose their own candidates rather than have new members imposed on them

6 How to Support your Team's Development

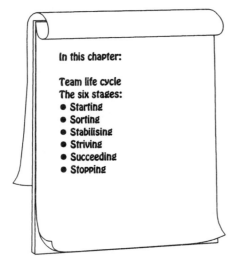

In this chapter:

Team life cycle
The six stages:
- Starting
- Sorting
- Stabilising
- Striving
- Succeeding
- Stopping

It's not much fun being a teenager with parents who don't understand you. The type of help and amount of understanding you receive can make growing up fun, a nightmare or just simply boring. Like individual human beings, teams grow up and eventually pass away. They have at least six phases in their natural development. By becoming aware of these phases, you can speed them up and help the team deal with them constructively.

Also as teenagers, there were probably moments when we felt extremely adult, on our way to total independence. Yet sometimes perhaps we briefly reverted to a state of dependency. Your team too may keep reaching one stage of development, only to revert to a previous one.

For example, just when you have everything working smoothly, a couple of team members may decide to leave. Until their replacements settle in, your team may be almost like a new one. Ways of working already settled may need airing again. Newcomers may not automatically acquire the team culture rapidly, or may be slow to grasp the ground rules.

It will probably save time in the long run to sort out relevant issues with the newcomers. Everything may need to be tackled, from 'we never miss deadlines in this team' to 'how we set our objectives'. By allowing this stage to reoccur, you speed up the integration of new team members, and it helps the rest of the team too.

A team's development is therefore not necessarily in a straight line, moving logically forward. The six stages of team development are: Starting, Sorting, Stabilising, Striving, Succeeding and Stopping.

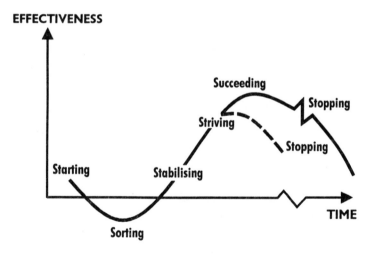

The developing team

The diagram of the developing team shows how the team's effectiveness may vary during its life cycle. Making the team aware of this process can often help people come to terms with what is happening. For example, the Sorting stage is often quite difficult, and may involve a considerable amount of conflict. During it the team is certainly not able to function at its best.

It may also be helpful for the team to understand that not all teams automatically reach the Success stage during which outstanding, even surprising results are achieved. Some teams never get this far, they merely remain competent. Discussions about what will move the team on to the Success stage are easier if everyone, not just the team leader, has a picture of the development cycle. This is illustrated as the life and death of a team.

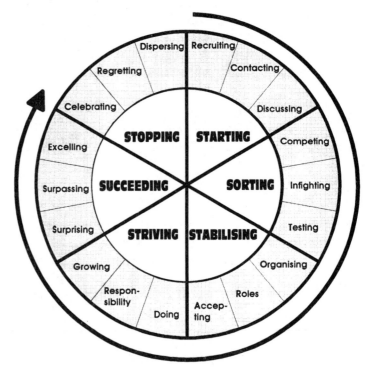

Life and death of a team

LEADERS NEED CONSTANTLY TO REVIEW

- What stage of development has the team reached?
- What work methods are we using?
- How can we move the team on to its next stage of development?

It is often unclear when one stage ends and another begins. What matters is developing your feel for what the team needs at any particular moment. Develop this by being alert to where the team might be in the development process, always checking what it requires to move on. Emergencies, for example, may cause a renewed period of Sorting and Stabilising. Help the team mature and experience the six stages by encouraging an emphasis on performance and constantly reminding it of the big picture — its vision and purpose.

During the six stages of a team's natural development its effectiveness may vary considerably. Energy levels may rise and fall and, with some justification, people may occasionally feel the team is not moving forward. This is a perfectly natural state of affairs: it is only damaging when the team gets stuck for a long time at a particular stage.

STARTING

A team begins with recruitment of the members, and this is also when everyone meets for the first time. If you can choose the membership, it may feel tempting to select people rather like you. However, what makes teams successful is diversity, not uniformity. So mixed gender teams are often more balanced and effective than all male or all female ones. Similarly, you need a team with a range of skills that together create 'more than the sum of the parts'.

At the start of a team's life, people naturally wonder how it will turn out. The unknown is usually worrying, so people may feel anxious. Be understanding of such feelings, they are perfectly natural.

STARTING

You can be inspiring if you:

- Help people get to know each other
- Declare what you want this team to be
- Share your vision of success
- Ask for people's initial thoughts on priorities
- Say what really matters to you about this team
- Offer guidance about purpose
- Avoid being over-directive or too assertive
- Convey a sense of confidence about what must be done

The creation of a new team is usually an exciting moment. It is your job to make it so. You can do this by offering a sense of direction. Collective energy may be high and the team will normally accept that you may not yet be entirely clear about how to get there. However, they will expect signs that you possess some picture or 'vision' of what the team is for, what you wish it to become.

Now is the time to give this stage of team development a push in the right direction by investing in some 'getting to know you' activities. This lays the ground work for better joint working in the future.

Time spent now on getting to know each other will repay you a hundredfold later. Rather than plunging straight into goals, deadlines, tasks, targets and responsibilities, devote space for people to connect. Letting this happen in the pub or in social activities is fine. There is also a considerable benefit in taking the team away for a day. Together you explore everyone's aspirations. Again, this approach works with British and American teams, but you may need to rethink it for a team from, say, France or Germany. At this stage you are the person most able to initiate the 'getting to know you' process.

Advice points

GETTING TO KNOW YOU

- Try asking the team in pairs to discover three areas where they differ significantly, perhaps outrageously, from each other

- Ask each team member to share with the team something they find inspiring — it could be a poem, a piece of music, an object

- Invite each member to say what three core values the team should live by and to offer examples of how they might recognise these values day to day

- By allowing time for team members to get to know each other, you are helping to promote trust

---

'Getting to know you' builds trust, awareness of each other's strengths and weaknesses, and begins to reduce interpersonal barriers. While you cannot force people to trust each other, you can create the conditions in which it flourishes.

There are many useful ways to accelerate the trust-building stage, some exciting and great fun. In our own work with teams we use many imaginative and amusing exercises drawn from the theatre and the performing arts. People try to discover strange facts about each other, they invent stories together, they jointly solve brainteasers and put on instant one-minute plays about the team. Theatre teams are used to building trust quickly and creating tightly knit teams fast. However, avoid forcing the pace, since people need time to get to grips with each other without excessive pressure.

The outward bound experience, for example, where people undertake risky and physically demanding activity, can sometimes work. Yet it is often difficult to carry over successfully to the workplace.

Your own leadership style will also matter a great deal at this stage. Given the uncertainty, it is easy to be over-directive, or too controlling. But despite this uncertainty, now is not the time to throw your weight around or to dominate.

Early in the team's life, most members want to show they can contribute. Make it easy for them to do so. One of your most positive contributions can be sharing your confidence in the new team, conveying an honest belief that together you can succeed.

Offering too many certainties now is seldom convincing. People know you do not have all the answers, so pretending otherwise is unhelpful. The challenge is achieving a balance between wanting to control the starting process, while allowing natural forces to work through. You will usually make a better contribution by creating opportunities for people to identify what tasks they might do. Part of this process is allowing time for them to probe each other's defences.

Now is also the time to begin setting goals that people can understand and that excite them. The team needs to be involved in discussing how to achieve them.

SORTING

The Sorting stage can be stormy, and uncomfortable for everyone. During it people want more clarification on everything, from values to roles, from tasks to the frequency of team meetings. As they confront over these issues, there may be infighting and jockeying for power. Members compete with each other rather than with outsiders. With frustration and anxiety quite high, energy levels may plummet.

It is usually a mistake to stop such conflicts from surfacing. They are part of the natural process of a team maturing. You can help by ensuring that the team acknowledges conflicts, does not over-personalise disagreements, and moves on. Despite such activity, or even because of it, some team members may become dispirited. How you handle this difficult period can even affect your longer-term success with the team. People are sizing you and each other up. What you do now sets the pattern for future team ways of working and influences performance.

While Sorting people may say:

Try to stay calm
Help the team select an
agenda of key tasks
Work to resolve any obvious
relationship problems
Focus on issues, not personalities
Schedule time for dealing
with any unresolved matters
Push for agreement on
roles and boundaries
Help people accept and
deal with conflict constructively

At this stage a major contribution you can make as a leader is providing reassurance. You do not need to gloss over the uncertainties or deny the risks. Yet simply by sharing your confidence in the future you will help the team move through the Sorting stage more smoothly.

Similarly, you need to model expected behaviour. At this stage people are still unsure of the exact forms of desirable behaviour and are looking for guidance. Don't necessarily give explicit instructions, often merely seeing how the team leader behaves is enough to inspire people to act appropriately.

So during this stage you can really contribute to the team's development if you show you are productive, are focused on quality of work, and demonstrate how to talk to people and customers. Likewise, when you model good listening behaviour you will be encouraging others to follow your lead.

STANDARDS

During the Sorting stage, help the team decide the standards it will adopt.

For example, David Gwynne became head of a team in a public service agency in Australia. He had no previous experience of such teams and learned it was normal practice for the longest-serving member to stand in during the team leader's absence.

However, he noticed that the person who normally did this also drank heavily in the lunch hour. So David called in the team member and put it simply: 'Look, what you do in your lunch hour is entirely your business. But returning with your breath smelling of alcohol is unacceptable and not pleasant for our clients. For the moment I am asking someone else to stand in for me.'

The team member was dumbfounded. He had simply never thought about this and immediately stopped his drinking during lunch hours. The rest of the team also got a clear message about standards.

STABILISING

You are at the Stabilising stage if there are now definite team ground rules or norms. Norms are 'how things should be around here'. They might include how we deal with disagreements, how closely we stick to deadlines, who substitutes during the leader's absence and so on.

Your team is now more organised, having dealt with many initial differences. There is growing clarity about what is to be done and how to do it. People are clearer, for instance, about their own roles or responsibilities. They also know broadly what other team members do and how they work. Sometimes you can help this stage of development along by some formal analysis of people's preferred roles. For example, some people like to offer lots of ideas, while others enjoy working on the team's behalf, obtaining information or resources.

Even if your own organisation is heavily committed to using job descriptions and formal task allocation, you may still need to adapt this to create your own approach. For example, the best teams are often ones where people are not over-constrained by their formal job titles or list of responsibilities. Instead they feel able to contribute in a whole variety of ways.

Ideally, aim to create a team of people willing to work flexibly, despite possibly inflexible job descriptions. By now the team is also starting to operate under a common set of values. Reinforce this by pressing for yet more clarity, by exploring issues such as: what are our core values and how are these lived out daily? Values are what the team really cares about. It needs to show these in action every day.

Values

Values are strongly held beliefs and are not easily altered. They might include ideas such as commitment to quality, getting it right first time, integrity, having fun, respect for people, openness, equality of opportunity, value for money, and so on. People say 'these are our values and we stand by them.'

This approach, however, may go down less well in

teams from a culture that is more akin to a family, in which personal relationships are far more important than systems or formal rules.

A team that says a core value is customer care does not just talk about it. It shows this in action every day. Values bind a team together when it is under pressure. Once established, they are unlikely to change much, and not without another, perhaps lengthy round of resorting and restabilising.

- Teams with clear values consistently outperform those without them
- Many traditional worries about team performance disappear when there are clear or accepted norms about how the team sees timeliness, cooperation, reliability and integrity

Norms

Norms are different to values. While norms are about 'the right way to do things around here', values are about our aspirations: 'How ideally we'd like it to be around here.' Because both are part of the warp and weft of the team's existence, they are often taken for granted.

When team members have successfully worked through the Stabilising stage norms are firmly entrenched. Consequently there is strong pressure to conform to them. To ignore a norm would call into question one's own team membership.

Collective energies rise during this stage as people begin accepting the requirements for being in this team. They accept certain tasks and roles as the price for being a team member. With many uncertainties resolved, people feel more able to start enjoying each other as work colleagues.

STRIVING

Now the team is really performing. Work is done, results are achieved. It is heading towards its vision and has important goals in sight. People feel productive and there is a reasonable degree of mutual trust. During it the team develops close working relationships. These carry it over or through many obstacles.

Like a top racing driver, you cannot expect to keep your foot permanently flat on the accelerator. Even during periods of great productivity, the team must occasionally slow down, if only to draw fresh breath for its next big effort.

STRIVING

- Support the actual work being done
- Keep the team focused
- Give regular rewards and feedback
- Watch for signs that enthusiasm is flagging
- Be ready to introduce fresh stimulus
- Find time for fun and non-work team activity
- Encourage people to take more responsibility
- Keep giving regular feedback about progress

A striving team is a competent one and widely respected. However, it is not yet a high flyer. Some teams never get beyond mere competence, and in many organisations that is perfectly acceptable.

One feature to look for in a striving team is how it handles risk. Those that are going beyond mere competence usually adopt a really positive attitude towards risk. People accept that playing safe will not take them much further.

SUCCEEDING

Only some teams reach this stage. A team is Succeeding when it consistently produces outstanding results, often against the odds. It makes the best use of everyone's potential.

Any team or company can do well if the conditions are right and the obstacles to market domination are small. In Britain during the 1980s and early 1990s the two or three largest supermarket chains had such huge leverage in the marketplace that their profits were always impressive.

With competition almost excluded, teams in these companies could afford to be competent, rather than outstanding. Inside one major player, for example, most of the emphasis was on control. Its internal teams seldom had to be creative or exploring.

With changes in the marketplace towards the mid-1990s, the big players began realising that mere competence was insufficient. Increasingly, they needed teams that went beyond the striving stage, ones able to succeed against the odds.

These teams would need to be more creative, risky, and able to learn from others. The leadership would also have to alter, giving more attention to getting the best from each member.

In Succeeding teams there is an urge for continuous improvement, people are always looking to reach the next level, the next goal, the next success. It is not that they are never satisfied, they just know there is always more to be done. There is an extremely high level of personal commitment from everyone. You can see this in those few companies that have put quality and customer satisfaction at the top of their agenda. Their adrenalin and energy levels are usually high and members approach their work expecting to overcome the most difficult and unexpected challenges.

HELPING THE TEAM REACH FOR SUCCESS

- Keep the focus on team performance — doing even better
- Encourage intensity of communication
- Promote interdependence between members
- Create pairs or small groups to solve problems
- Ask for formal presentations on how to tackle issues
- Provide resources and encouragement for team growth
- Act as a team player yourself
- Approach every task as an opportunity for teamwork
- Rely on commitment, rather than control
- Put more emphasis on team than individual rewards
- Tap each person's potential through work challenges, regular training and career development

In a Succeeding team you can rely less on controlling people and more on personal commitment. For example, in these winning teams people thrive on autonomy and challenge, rather than constant direction. It is a difficult balance to strike. On the one hand you want everyone working closely together, with as little damaging interpersonal competition as possible. Yet you also want them acting on their own initiative, taking responsibility.

The higher you go in conventional organisations, the greater the conflict seems, since large egos are hard to harness. Too often, top teams are merely a collection of individuals going through the motions of joint working. In our consulting work, for instance, we often find top managers claiming 'we are a great team', only to discover that the reality is entirely different.

To challenge and give autonomy while avoiding over-controlling behaviour means finding the right balance by trial and error. In such teams you often cannot easily detect who is the leader: occasionally everyone appears leader-like.

Since people in a Succeeding team usually know more about their specific jobs than you do, you become highly dependent on them, rather than the other way around. Control is therefore less effective for producing results than is relying on inherent commitment. You now rely heavily on the members deciding for themselves what needs to be done, what is a priority and how to use resources.

The work environment of many Succeeding teams is often unstable. They constantly face new situations, yet people need to respond flexibly. This will only occur if you are constantly developing each person. It is why companies like Motorola and SmithKline Beecham have launched what they have called universities, dedicated to helping everyone grow as human beings.

While growth is not easy to define, you know it when you see it. Grow the person and you grow the team, and the organisation. To inspire a Succeeding team means taking a real interest in people's training and development needs. This is how you keep encouraging them to do even better, to make a bigger contribution, to be more creative and proactive.

STOPPING

One day the team must end. Few effective teams last indefinitely. Some struggle on in the minds of the members, even after disbanding. Those that continue when they have long since ceased to be Striving or Succeeding normally turn into committees. Long-running boards of directors easily degenerate this way, losing the vital spark that once made them powerful, unless they are constantly waking themselves up and renewing their energy. When they fail to do this, such top teams tend to retreat into having ritual meetings where nothing much important happens.

Occasionally a team stops, only to start again in a new form. Maybe some team members leave, the roles change or the team has an entirely new challenge to revitalise it.

SETTING A STOP DATE

Set definite ending dates for project teams. If necessary, form a new one to complete the mopping-up arrangements. People like to feel the team's work will be completed, rather than drift on indefinitely.

A project group in a computer company had long ago completed the bulk of its original work. Because there was still mopping up to do, the whole team was retained. With no end date in sight, energy and commitment were extremely low.

A new team leader diagnosed the situation and told the project team he was setting a definite time for the team to end. He explained that an entirely fresh taskforce would complete any outstanding work after that date. With an end in sight, people were more able to put energy into the remaining work.

How you handle the closing period is important, otherwise you could leave a legacy of discontent that returns to haunt your future work. For example, where appropriate, use the ending as an opportunity to celebrate your time together.

Recognise too, that many team members may be feeling sad or angry at stopping. They may also have mixed emotions about it. There may be relief, but also perhaps sadness. The greater the team's success, the more intense the sense of loss. Acknowledge and deal with these feelings.

Disbanding may be quite traumatic, reactions may be similar to mourning a real death: disbelief, bewilderment, anger, resignation, sadness, renewed hope. Help the team by acknowledging these feelings, and allow time to work through them.

As leader you are likely to be in the best position to detect the Stopping stage coming over the horizon. By spending time preparing, you will certainly handle the whole experience more confidently. Consequently people who have worked in the team may remember your handling of the closure, and be more willing to join a team led by you in the future.

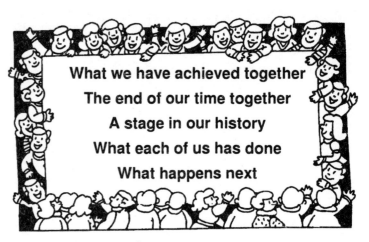

What we have achieved together

The end of our time together

A stage in our history

What each of us has done

What happens next

Celebrating: Making endings more acceptable

ACTION POINTS

 Stay aware of what is happening in your team

 Anticipate problems and remove blocks to better working

 Keep reviewing what stage the team has reached

 Clarify what roles people are playing

 Use the six stages of team development to guide you

 Share with your team the natural stages of team development

 Build trust in the team

 Create opportunities for people to identify tasks and behaviours they will perform

 Allow room for people to probe each other's

defences, and learn what matters to those with whom they will be working

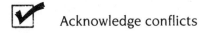 Acknowledge conflicts

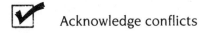 Deal with conflict by focusing on issues, not personalities

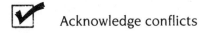 Clarify the team's core values and what they mean in practice

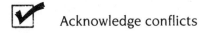 Help enforce ground rules for working together

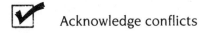 Show your personal commitment to the ground rules

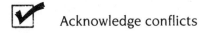 Keep the team energies focused

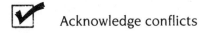 Give regular rewards and feedback

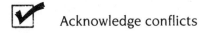 Use commitment rather than control to obtain high-level results

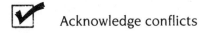 When it is time to end the team set a definite ending date

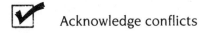 Acknowledge and deal with people's feelings about ending the team

 Celebrate or formally mark the ending of a team

7 How to Review Your Team's Progress

Prime Ministers do it. So do football managers. Anyone responsible for a team needs occasionally to stand back from the daily maelstrom and take a long look at how it is doing. In cabinets there are reshuffles. In football teams they sell players or move them to new positions. In organisations team reviews mean anything from a new direction to the team's demise.

Why bother? Even if you think the team is doing fine, the team review is like a regular health check. While you may not need one, it makes definite sense to have one occasionally. The older the team the more sensible it is to explore 'how are we doing?'

TEAM REVIEWS

- Identify blocks to team working
- Resolve interpersonal problems
- Give the team fresh momentum
- Provide new direction
- Keep the team fresh
- Inspire people
- Improve commitment
- Help understand what is happening
- Revive a thirst for growth and change
- Restimulate a hunger for the next big target
- Refocus attention on the big (strategic) picture

A team review focuses on issues not normally dealt with in day-to-day progress meetings. It is mainly about how people are working together — the team processes. Well-run reviews therefore strengthen the team, and at worst fail to make much difference. It is rare for one to turn sour or cause real damage. It is the lack of a review that usually proves to be most damaging.

Yet some teams and their leaders avoid ever holding a review in any depth. This often stems from fear. Fear of whether the team can handle a close look at itself, fear of damaging personal relationships, fear of damage to the team leader's authority.

TEAM REVIEWS

- The team leader needs to discover from team members — How can I help you do your jobs better?
- Team members need to learn from the leader — How can we help you be more effective?
- The team tries to discover — How can we obtain better results together?

Advice points

A review is a powerful FORCE for change and inspiration if it is:

- Fun
- Open
- Regular
- Challenging
- Energising

FUN

Make the review an enjoyable, learning experience rather than merely another chore. With good planning you can make it creative, enjoyable and stimulating. Strangely, not everyone sees such aims as desirable.

Some people, for example, regard it as frivolous for fun to permeate work. This is losing sight of how people learn and grow. A review need not be a deadly serious affair. Making it into an ordeal stops people feeling stimulated or deters them from making worthwhile contributions.

Try asking the team for its ideas if you are unsure how to inject some fun. They will usually produce plenty of suggestions, if convinced you will take notice.

Be wary of requests for the team to spend its review time on adventure games or in physical activity of a demanding nature. While these can certainly be fun for some people, it can be hard to integrate the experience into the review process. It may also make little difference back in the workplace.

A team can have fun while still being fully engaged in a serious review process. For example, the managing director of an EMAP publishing company once got her team to dress up in Star Trek uniforms. Their mission was to explore how 'we can boldly go where no team has gone before'.

Similarly, the Tricorn design company regularly hires conference premises nearby in the Chessington World of Adventures. During breaks, team members wander off and enjoy the rides. They return flushed and laughing, ready for another session on improving how they work together.

OPEN

The whole point of a review is sharing what is happening and using it to improve performance. During it, people are frank about saying what they think. This requires a climate in which people feel safe to speak, which depends on how the review is set up and run. Experienced team helpers, for example, can rapidly create the sense of safety that encourages openness.

Unwittingly, you as the team leader may be a reason that people do not feel entirely safe to say what they think. This may have nothing to do with your personality. In a strongly hierarchical organisation, or in a professional practice with senior and junior partners, a formal role can set you slightly apart.

An outside team facilitator reduces this unwanted impact by using ways to blur the boundaries temporarily, without affecting your formal authority. Briefly suspending hierarchical arrangements has great benefits. Team members who have taken part in a review often say the suspension of the hierarchy, although only brief, was the most rewarding part of the experience.

An important way you can contribute to more openness is by being willing to raise issues that might in some way be against yourself: for example, how the leader handles meetings. By modelling openness you encourage it in others.

REGULAR

A team review has added power when it occurs at regular intervals. Teams often hit a plateau when they feel understimulated and uninterested. Regular reviews ensure there is not too much gap before time is spent on helping the team tackle such issues.

Once the team knows you support a regular review, many issues that might otherwise become more pressing can be safely postponed until it occurs. Reviews therefore save the team time. Otherwise these issues simply clog up normal meetings.

Make the review frequent enough for each event to build on the previous one. With a short-life team — say under three months — half a day is probably enough. For a permanent or long-lasting team, quarterly reviews of at least a day are a sound investment.

By building the review into normal working practice you can avoid springing it on the team. People look forward to it and plan their time around it.

CHALLENGING

Many issues may never surface during normal team contact. Pressure of work may be one cause, reluctance to confront may be another. The longer you wait before undertaking a team review, the more such issues accumulate. Often team leaders know certain subjects have been ignored. However, they may also fear that once these are on the agenda they or the team may be unable to handle them. This is rarely the case. Like a boil that needs lancing, once issues are tackled the team will feel and act differently.

It is usually better to face issues that cause team conflict than simply ignore them. In genuine teams people rely on each other and this trust develops because of a readiness to tackle such blocks. Otherwise issues can only explode during normal working and undermine teamwork. An effective review always poses real challenges.

Personal grievances against each other

Feelings of powerlessness

Disatisfaction with allocation of work

Insufficient sharing of information

Competitive behaviour

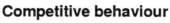

Anger at decisions

Celebrate success

Frustration about some past incident

Failure to receive support

Resentment at lack of appreciation or recognition

Neglected issues that reviews may need to tackle

ENERGISING

The team review is a great place to reenergise the team. Often it will only require half a day together talking about non-operational issues to trigger off new levels of enthusiasm and drive.

Energy is such a critical factor in a team's success that you need never apologise for devoting time away from day-to-day work to explore how to maintain and increase it.

Successful reviews do not necessarily address the energy issue head on. Often it is enough simply to devote time away from the work scene to other aspects of team development. However, there may be occasions when you should direct the team's attention to its current level of energy and obtain people's views on what it will take to alter that.

Inspiring team leaders manage to tap into people's energy reserves, even when these are low. Team reviews are an important resource for doing this, since the break away from work can itself provide a focus for new energy. People remind themselves of what the work is really about, of things that matter, like team values, and what everyone aspires to — the vision.

The different stages of a team's development (see Chapter 6) mean that there are periods when it is understandable for energy levels to drop. For example, during the Sorting stage of development, members may become so frustrated with conflict and interpersonal competition that team energy falls dramatically. When you conduct a team review, you begin to reverse this fall.

Successful reviews therefore leave people feeling energised, more committed both to each other and team goals. You ensure this in many different ways. For example, through dealing with accumulated 'baggage', removing blocks to thinking and communicating, tapping into people's creativity, strengthening interpersonal relationships, and posing fresh challenges.

TOOLS FOR CONDUCTING REVIEWS

How do you systematically obtain a clear picture of the team's current strengths and development needs? Posing a general question such as 'how are we doing?' may not necessarily provide the answers.

Although there are many ways of conducting a systematic review, two important ones are exploring the role each member plays; and discovering how the team handles its work — team processes.

A popular method is to look at team characteristics. For example, the role each person plays or prefers to play. Such roles may be formal, such as one's professional function — accountant, solicitor, engineer, sales manager and so on. It could be an informal role such as an ideas person, or a chairperson.

ROLES

People take informal roles because they like them, or because the team has seen them that way. For example, one member may become known for helping to resolve conflict, or another may be particularly good at chairing meetings, doing so without being even asked.

Exploring roles can stimulate a team to start talking about issues of effectiveness. However, fixed roles cease to be entirely relevant when a team is in trouble, or highly productive. During periods of tension and pressure the labels may no longer make much sense. Role is therefore only one dimension of a team.

By exploring how your team functions together, you can begin to alter its ultimate performance. There are various ways of doing this, although this is not yet a fully developed area. Some processes are described in the following section.

WORK METHODS — TEAM PROCESSES

ACE TEAMS

In the diagram on page 106 there are 10 important team processes which describe a successful team, one that is Aligned, Creative and Exploring: an ACE team. Many

Aligned

Aligned Leadership	Incisive Organisation	Supportive Relationships	Personal Investment
Clear values	Right membership	Supportive	Personal connection
Committed to values	Clear objectives	Sharing	Satisfaction
Powerful vision	Commitment to objectives	Trust	Responsibility
Clear leadership	Timescales	Feelings	Reputation on the line
Loyalty to the leadership	Highly organised working	Respect for the individual	Use abilities

Creative

Permissive Encouragement	Creative Energy	Using the whole person
'Yes' Culture	Rocking the boat	Physical energy
Experimenting	Play and fun	Mentally stretched
Constructive disagreement	Sense of humour	Emotional expression
Building on ideas	Ups and downs	Respect for intuition
Permission to fail	Honesty	Work excites

Exploring

Spirit of Adventure	Growth and Discovery	Wholehearted Appreciation
Push for impact	Regular assessment	Recognition
Peak performance	Feedback	Receive appreciation
Careful preparation	Keeping fresh	Spontaneity
Channelled energy	Fighting routine	Formal celebrations
Risk taking	Opposition and challenge	Encouragement not criticism

teams manage to become strong on one or two of these dimensions. Far fewer develop strengths in all three.

An Aligned team is the first base that a team must reach if it is to be fully successful. A team is strongly aligned when it has Aligned Leadership, Incisive Organisation, Supportive Relationships and Personal Investment — people really putting all of themselves into the work.

ALIGNED TEAMS

Aligned leadership is one of the most important aspects of a well-run team. There are clear values to which everyone is committed. There is also usually a powerful vision behind what people are doing. At most times, there is certainty about who is leading, though this may not always be the formally appointed leader.

Aligned Leadership

People also feel a strong loyalty to the leadership. Such loyalty might surface in many ways, for example in backing the leader when times are difficult, or in not taking part in malicious gossip about the leadership.

When the team is strongly aligned you will find that it is *incisively organised*. You recognise this is happening when the team has clearly recruited the right members who are working well together. There are clear objectives that everyone understands and to which they are committed. Incisive organisation also means the team works to clear and tight timescales.

Incisive Organisation

There are also *supportive relationships* in strongly aligned teams. You know this because people help each other in various ways, from offering encouragement to being good at listening, from plunging in to help someone in difficulties to backing them up in meetings. There is therefore considerable sharing in an aligned team.

Supportive Relationships

For example, rather than hoarding information, people readily share it with each other. Considerable trust also exists. Even if team members do not actually meet that often, they have a great deal of faith in their colleagues and can rely on them.

As you might expect, in a team showing supportive

relationships feelings are expressed openly, and widely recognised as an important resource for improving communications and joint working. It is not that the team keeps obsessively focusing on feelings. It merely makes it acceptable to express them, and people respond positively when someone does so.

Ultimately, the sure sign of an aligned team with supportive relationships is when you see the members thoroughly respecting one another. They show this in many ways, from not interrupting to how they talk to each other. Respect for the individual also means the team acknowledges people's differences and really values these.

Personal Investment

In a strongly aligned team there is a high level of *personal investment* by the members. People not only put all of themselves into the work, they also feel powerfully connected to one another, even without meeting frequently. This sense of connection is a source of great personal satisfaction to team members. People really enjoy what they do and think it is worthwhile.

With a high level of personal investment everyone seems willing to put their own reputations on the line. They take responsibility for what they do, expecting to be judged by how they do it. Such a team uses everyone's abilities to the full. People will usually tell you they feel fully stretched and personally challenged.

Responsibility for developing an aligned team rests with everyone, not just the formal leader. So it is important for the whole team to understand how they can help achieve it. The various components of aligned leadership, incisive organisation and so on make effective issues to consider in depth, at regular team assessments.

CREATIVE TEAMS

You know your team is strongly Creative if there is Permissive Encouragement, Creative Energy, and Use of the Whole Person. All these elements need to exist, not just one or two of them.

There is *permissive encouragement* when the team exhibits a 'yes' culture where people greet new ideas, suggestions and proposals positively. So, for example, rather than usually responding to suggestions with 'Yes but...', they are more open minded, willing to search for ways to make it happen.

In the spirit of a 'yes' culture, creative teams are keen experimenters. They are constantly testing the limits of what is possible, they keep trying out new ideas and willingly discard ones that do work. Naturally in such teams there are regular disagreements, since people are different and have their own perspective on situations. However, disagreements in a strongly creative team are not destructive, since people are personally damaged or attacked when these differences of opinion surface.

Instead, disagreements are treated as a powerful tool for achieving high-level results. So when there is dissent, it is normally constructive disagreement. One practical way this occurs is that each person builds on what the previous person has said, rather than just waiting their turn to talk.

So during meetings, for example, people do not knock what the last person has just said. Instead they will acknowledge the contribution and try to develop it. In creative teams, therefore, everyone listens with their full attention.

Aligned teams expect to succeed, yet permissive encouragement also gives people permission to fail. This is not a licence for continued poor performance. It is public recognition that team members will only grow and develop by learning through their mistakes. Creative teams therefore avoid penalising people for their failures, instead asking questions such as 'What did you learn from this?' or 'How could we avoid this happening again?'

As you might expect in a strongly creative team, there is a great deal of *creative energy* around. This is not vague, frenetic activity with members trying to show they are really busy. Where there is creative energy people are

Permissive Encouragement

Creative Energy

willing to rock the boat, challenge conventions and ask questions like 'is there a better way?' This openness can be difficult for some organisations to tolerate, especially those that are strong on control, rather than empowerment.

Creative energy also abounds when people feel able to play together, having fun as a team. This can mean anything from telling jokes in team meetings to enjoying each other's company over a drink, or solving a problem. While the team may regard its actual work as important, it rarely takes itself too seriously.

A willingness to make room for play and fun can seem frivolous to some people. 'Our managers are very serious people' is how one personnel expert described to us the nature of her senior hierarchy. She clearly felt the people concerned would reject out of hand any idea of play and fun. An important contribution leaders, trainers and outsiders can often make to teams is helping them relearn how play and fun get people working well together. Similarly, in teams with plenty of creative energy, there is usually a good sense of humour, people laugh together and are willing to see the funny side of life. This ability to use humour is much neglected in organisations and remains a powerful force for finding creative solutions and making new ideas more acceptable.

Creative teams are always making things happen around them, so they are usually in a constant state of change. We like to call it the roller coaster effect. Since no individual or team can stay energised the whole time, there are inevitably barren periods. Strongly creative teams understand the need for these periods in the wilderness. They accept them as the price paid for those glorious moments when together they hit the peaks.

You always find a great deal of honesty where there are high levels of creative energy. Team members speak frankly to each other and do not deliberately conceal their meanings or work to hidden agendas. Instead people say what they think, without attempting to manipulate others for their own ends. Of course team members use persuasion and influence to achieve what they want. In a team with a great deal of honesty, however, it is done openly and with good will.

Using the Whole Person

Strongly creative teams use every part of each person, not just one skill or ability. So for example, people are not merely mentally stretched. They are also able to use the full range of their emotional expression if they choose to do so.

Using the whole person also means using people's physical energy, perhaps encouraging unexpected opportunities for this to occur. For example, a group of clients in the Stock Exchange once challenged our company team to participate in a game of softball. We welcomed this as a chance to use a part of ourselves the ordinary day-to-day teamwork would not normally employ.

A particularly important aspect of teams using the whole person is their respect for people's natural intuition. There is widespread recognition among the members that 'gut feel', instinct and intuitive flair are valuable creative resources. This respect may seem strange to those trained to demand hard evidence, and only to rely on measuring things. Yet intuition is how we make many vital decisions, even when we have collected large amounts of information. Intuition taps part of ourselves that at some unexplained level already 'knows' the answer. It is partly a matter of trust.

In areas where the team is trying to invent new ways of working, or solve creative challenges, intuition is as important as knowledge or technical analysis. It is combining intuition with other more conventional means that usually proves the most effective approach.

People are excited in strongly creative teams, becoming stimulated by the whole process. This in turn increases the amount of creative energy. A sense of excitement is infectious: when people regard their work in that way they attract others who want to help them succeed.

Finally, a team that is strong on Exploring shows a Spirit of Adventure, Growth and Discovery, and Wholehearted Appreciation.

Spirit of Adventure

This is when the team often reaches beyond its own boundaries to discover what impact it can make in new areas. You can recognise a powerful and attractive *spirit of adventure* from various signs. For example, the team pushes hard to make an impact, it really wants to make a difference in the world.

Such a team does not merely want to make a sale, for instance. It also wants the sale to be of real benefit to the customer. Exploring teams are always concerned with adding value. Such teams will go the extra mile, looking for ways to surprise customers and discovering how they can excite colleagues. These teams are not merely successful, they also regularly achieve peak performance.

Peak performance in these teams is incredibly impressive. You see people pushing themselves to their limits, always asking 'How can we do it even better?' Occasionally these teams hit such a stride, they cannot seem to put a foot wrong, apparently going from strength to strength. The secret is not entirely mysterious. It's grounded firmly in careful preparation, often lasting years rather than months. Exploring teams do not merely plan well, they keep evaluating the progress of their plans, continually adjusting performance to the changing situation and environment.

Behind their spirit of adventure is also a deliberate channelling of energy. These teams have a strong focus, directing their attention and efforts like a laser beam on maximum power. There is little or no evidence of wasted energy, since people are constantly aware of what they are doing and why.

The price these teams pay for their spirit of adventure is that they are unashamed risk takers. To explore beyond the team boundaries and make a significant impact means tackling new, large, and often unknown territory. With such uncertainty goes risk. But risk taking is responsible, not reckless. The team rarely if ever 'bets the farm', jeopardises its own existence or that of the enterprise. Risks are merely part of discovering what is possible.

Growth and Discovery

Growth and discovery are shown by the team's willingness to assess regularly how it is doing. It does not look for comfortable reassurance that everything is fine. Instead it goes out of its way to uncover how it is seen by its fellow teams, by customers, and by those at higher levels in the organisation.

Such teams are therefore keen on promoting regular feedback, both from within and from beyond their own boundaries. They may encourage this in many ways, from informal meetings inviting opinions to formal surveys and studies.

A team that is strong on growth and discovery will also consciously seek to keep itself fresh, constantly looking for ways to renew its energy and ideas. Not surprisingly, such teams fight routine and do not always play by the accepted rules long established in an organisation. They thrive on opposition and challenge. While not necessarily courting opposition, their drive to make an impact and their constant desire to stay fresh mean they seldom sit still for long. They use opposition and challenge constructively to learn and develop.

Wholehearted Appreciation

In these teams there is *wholehearted appreciation* that often goes well beyond the natural confines of the group. For example, in strongly exploring teams there is usually a hunger for widespread recognition by peer groups, by customers, by the world at large.

This desire for recognition is not infantile. It is a natural one for any team wanting to make a significant impact beyond its own narrow boundaries. When recognition and appreciation do come, the team accepts these with pleasure, rather than dismissing or taking them for granted.

Another important way that the exploring team handles appreciation is through its natural spontaneity.

Team members give recognition and praise, often without planning it in advance. People look for and take every opportunity to give others appreciation.

There are also formal celebrations. These may be anything from reward ceremonies to parties, from away days to a night at the theatre. Exploring teams look for excuses to celebrate. They will always mark a big event, such as a large sale or the end of a project. In our own company, for example, we have visited several shows in town just to celebrate our enjoyment in working together and as a reward for everyone's commitment.

Above all, wholehearted appreciation in the exploring team means encouragement not criticism. Often this will challenge members to find ways to be encouraging when the temptation may really be to find fault. It is through encouragement that the team grows and feels able to keep testing its boundaries.

MEASURING EFFECTIVENESS

Long-term measures such as profitability, turnover, sales, output and so on are traditionally how we tend to judge a team's effectiveness. The trouble is, by the time such information is available for examination, it is often too late to do much about it.

Using the ACE team framework you can assess your team while it is performing, rather than afterwards. For example, in the diagram on page 115 we show the profile of the Pavilion Team, in which each team member has completed a brief questionnaire, either on paper or directly onto a computer. The information enables people to share their current view of the team.

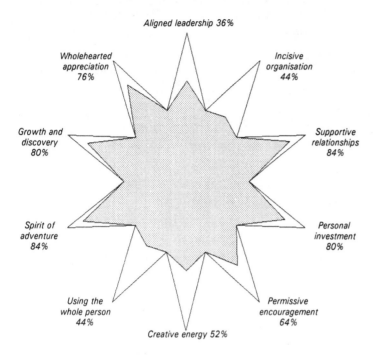

Aligned leadership 36%

Wholehearted
appreciation
76%

Incisive
organisation
44%

Growth and
discovery
80%

Supportive
relationships
84%

Spirit of
adventure
84%

Personal
investment
80%

Using the
whole person
44%

Permissive
encouragement
64%

Creative energy 52%

The Pavilion Ace team profile

The ACE Team framework focuses attention on how the
Pavilion team is working together. For example, it is
apparent that this particular team is particularly weak on
aligned leadership and could be much more incisively
organised. It is also possible to produce separate team
profiles as seen by each member of the team. This
provides an interesting comparative picture. For instance,
a leader may believe the team is strong on aligned
leadership, only to discover this is not how separate
team members see it.

ACE TEAM ASSESSMENT

A benefit of measuring a team's effectiveness is creating hard evidence on which to pursue joint action. In Sun Alliance Assurance, for example, internal organisational consultant Sue Petitt faced a team that was initially reluctant to take a rigorous look at itself and its performance.

She persuaded the team to complete an ACE Teams questionnaire and invited them to discuss the results. Because they had some numerical evidence describing their effectiveness, the team became more willing to go deeper, to review its ways of working.

In the Ladbroke Group, management development manager Ann Edwards wanted a way of comparing the different views of individuals towards their team and of analysing the team's effectiveness. The ACE Teams profile allowed her to 'catch people's thoughts and feelings and look at task direction and the uncertainties. It was a useful point for discussion and could take groups further into team building.'

In the Medway area of Kent, three different medical practices explored their team working by drawing up their ACE Team profile. Members of the practices spent two days in a hotel examining their joint working using the team profile to help focus thinking on priorities for change. Based on the profiles and other work, the teams drew up detailed action plans for change

With the ACE Teams approach you can also use the computer to create a detailed written report about the team that interprets the profile and offers specific suggestions for action. This report complements the skills of the leader or a trainer in giving guidance.

One benefit of using a regular assessment of how a team is working together is the ability to repeat it at regular intervals. Unlike a review of roles, an assessment of team processes is likely to keep providing new information. Previous assessments also make a good baseline on which to judge how the team is changing.

You can also learn more ACE Teams in our book
ACE Teams: Creating Star Performance in Business
(Butterworth Heinemann, 1994). See also Chapter 14,
Team Characteristics.

ACTION POINTS

 The older the team, the more sensible it is to explore 'how are we doing?'

 Try to keep the team assessment focused on total performance, rather than day-to-day problems

 Make your assessments have FORCE, by making them fun, open, regular, challenging, energising

 During team assessments find a way to eliminate the hierarchy briefly

 Consider using an outside facilitator to help steer a team assessment

 Build the assessment process into normal working practice

 Ensure assessments tackle challenging issues

 Consider using a formalised measurement system for assessing the team's strengths and weaknesses

 To assess team effectiveness consider checking on how far it is Aligned, Creative and Exploring

8 How to Ask for the Moon and Get it

'Kids, we must ship the product before the snow falls.' This was how Steve Ballmer of Microsoft galvanised his team of programmers to get the new Windows software onto the shelves by the end of the year. Dedication became fanaticism. Gabe Newall, a Windows tester, reportedly arrived at the office with a sleeping bag. For a month he bedded down in his office, working around the clock. From then on, they called him 'Mad Newall'.

LEADERS UNLOCK POTENTIAL BY:

- Sharing vision and values
- Valuing people
- Giving feedback and recognition
- Offering minimal criticism
- Fostering creativity
- Stretching people's talents
- Managing aspirations

Motivation is not something you *do* to people, since they already possess it. The challenge is to release it, for the benefit of the whole team, by some of the actions described below.

SHARED VISION AND VALUES

Behind most exceptional teams is a shared vision and common set of values. So what is a vision? When a new chief executive took over at award-winning Braintree Council, her initial reaction to the high-flown words about vision was 'it was management gobbledegook'. Gradually though, she came to realise the council was serious about its vision of service to the community.

A vision is what the team aspires to. Some visions may never be entirely achievable. Yet their very existence can inspire or excite people — especially if there is real effort to turn them into a reality. Where the vision comes from is less important than whether team members fully share it.

While it is not hard to check whether a common team vision exists, many team leaders do not bother. They assume everyone already shares the same view because, for example, there has been an agreed brief or set of objectives.

Where does a vision come from? Do you have it suddenly one morning, on the train travelling to work? How does a team leader go about creating an attractive vision? Essentially it stems from what you value or care strongly about. President Kennedy used his vision of Americans landing on the moon as a way of expressing his hopes for the country. Having decided what mattered he 'sold' his vision to the nation as getting there by the end of the decade.

Values therefore underpin the vision. There are normally only a few values. Each person can usually identify and explain them in their own words. They are not necessarily the same as written mission statements or slogans on office walls.

ALLIED DUNBAR CORE VALUES

Swindon-based Allied Dunbar Assurance decided to become more focused around its customers' needs. To help its many teams get to grips with the new values of its more market-led approach, the company identified the personality or reputation it wanted to establish:

- Genuine care
- Open, honest and direct
- Knowledgeable and experienced
- Energetic and enthusiastic
- Always helpful and responsive
- Confront issues
- Can be trusted

An important role you can play as a team leader is regularly to restate team values and display them in action, by what you do. Similarly, ask team members to keep producing examples of how they are making the values live.

VALUING PEOPLE

An important reason someone will work exceptionally hard is because they feel you value them as a person. You do this by treating each person with respect and by persisting in demanding that this is how team members treat each other too.

HOW TO VALUE EACH PERSON IN THE TEAM

Provide a worthwhile role by:

- giving people meaningful tasks
- confirming that what they do really matters
- delegating fully

Recognise people's efforts by:

- showing your appreciation when people try hard
- regularly thanking people for their contributions
- acknowledging people's successes

Listen to people carefully by:

- giving your full attention through active listening
- showing by your response that you have listened
- encouraging people to say what they think

Speak to people with respect by:

- treating each person as important
- accepting that each person has a point of view
- not impugning a person's motives

Discover how people are feeling by:

- seeking a personal response
- asking for their instinctive reactions
- paying attention to emotions

Express concern about their welfare by:

- showing you care if people have problems
- offering help in difficult times
- asking how they are getting on

Ensure their work is valued by others by:

- telling others what the person has done
- offering public praise and recognition

FEEDBACK

Research in many organisations confirms that there is seldom enough recognition. People too often feel taken for granted and there is insufficient feedback about their efforts. Recognition does not always need to be in money or a promotion. Like actors needing applause, your team wants clear signs of appreciation. This can be through saying 'thank you', a small gift, public praise, a party and so on.

"Once in a century a man may be ruined or made insufferable by praise. But surely once in a minute something generous dies for want of it. **"**
(John Masefield)

CREATIVITY

Creativity is one of the most powerful means of unlocking your team's full potential and releasing new energy. You can foster creativity by being open to new possibilities, new connections, surprising solutions. To use everyone in the team fully, they need to be stretched as human beings. This means not so much impossible goals as making huge demands on each person.

ENCOURAGE TEAM CREATIVITY THROUGH:

- Constantly experimenting
- Avoiding premature criticism of new ideas
- Welcoming suggestions
- Using creativity techniques regularly
- Handling periods of change in the creative process
- Offering large challenges

To make such demands you need to know each person's talents. You can find these out in many ways, such as formal assessment procedures, asking the person, asking others, through trial and error in the workplace, and so on. The range of your team's talents may prove surprising. For example, someone may have a gift for

PRAISE

Offer it regularly
Let it be honest
Make it personal
Sometimes make it public
Make it specific
Look pleased when giving it

languages yet never use it at work. Someone else may be adept at networking yet never help the rest of the team develop their skills in this area.

Advice points

HAVING FUN UNCOVERING TALENTS

Give everyone 10 cards. Ask them to list on each card a particular talent they possess. These do not need to be all work related. Ask people to initial each card.

Collect the cards and mix them up. Ask someone to read each card aloud and give the team three guesses to identify who owns that particular talent.

If necessary, use the initial on the card to reveal the owner of the talent.

INSPIRING THAT SPECIAL EFFORT

People will do extraordinary work for some team leaders and not for others. The ones who extract heroic effort, express vividly what is at stake. People therefore come to see their own interests as linked to what the leader wants to achieve.

When you call for a special team effort, people respond to facts *and* emotion. Both are essential. Facts start the process of convincing your team that outstanding effort is essential. Prepare any such facts carefully since they must to stand up to scrutiny.

TELL YOUR TEAM:

- The situation
- Why a Herculean effort is essential
- The exact results expected
- How long the exceptional effort might be needed
- The implications of succeeding
- The price of failure
- You want their help

Emotion is the other essential ingredient. You must appeal to people's feelings, not just their logical, rational

CRTISISM

Avoid it, or do it rarely
Ensure it's constructive
Do it in private
Make it fair
Give examples
Offer it without anger

part. Facts alone seldom tap a team's special reserves of energy and commitment.

It is the emotional side of your own personality combined with solid facts that will strike the spark. Through sharing your true feelings people realise that a great effort is unavoidable. This can be a difficult personal challenge. It may even feel alien and 'unprofessional' to resort to emotions to get what you want. To convince people at an emotional level means showing your own emotions. Unless you feel strongly about this special effort, why should they?

If you succeed in triggering a special effort you also need to sustain it for long enough to achieve the exceptional goal. You can rely on two distinct approaches: the slave driver solution, and the Moses appeal.

Slave driver solution

Slave drivers extract outstanding effort by ruthlessly pushing everyone to their limits and beyond. They cajole, threaten, promise, argue, and generally make outrageous demands. They brook no opposition to sustaining a special team effort.

Nor do slave drivers worry much about any damage done to the team, only about what the team will do for them. Although they get results, their method produces diminishing returns. It may succeed the first time, particularly if it takes the team by surprise. Later though, the response may be weaker and increasingly short lived.

Although slave drivers may offer rewards for exceptional effort, these seldom make much impact. The team is usually more concerned about being bullied, harassed and threatened. Avoidance of pain rather than the attraction of something pleasant underpins this approach.

Slave drivers usually forget to switch off, extending their method to everyday work. This further reduces their ability to command a much needed exceptional effort. Instinctively, the team protects itself by discovering ways to reduce the leader's power to tyrannise.

Slave driving works badly when team members owe no

particular loyalty to the leader. For example, many project and assignment teams are drawn from different departments, or even organisations. The team leader may have only limited power to threaten people's personal interests.

Using the Moses appeal, you rely on persuasion, inspiration, challenge, assurances, requests and disapprovals. Like Moses leading his people to the promised land, you depend on creating followers, who mainly come willingly.

Moses appeal

This method is more readily repeatable than slave driving. It is easier to help the team along through encouragement than constantly trying to drive it. There may be the occasional threat, through for example revealing the consequences of failure. It may also mean showing disapproval when the team is not making the necessary exertion.

You avoid picking on individuals who are not doing enough at this critical time. Instead you 'reward' individual effort with frequent recognition and praise. You look for any sign that people are making the special effort required and immediately 'reinforce' this by offering approval and acknowledgement.

YOUR OWN WAY

Experiment to discover what will call forth and sustain a short-lived, outstanding effort from your particular team. Sometimes the team itself is your best adviser. Ask the members what they feel would trigger a truly outstanding effort.

Whether you adopt the slave driver solution or the Moses appeal, or more likely a mixture of both, you need to develop a method that suits your own style. When you need a special team effort, this is the moment for showing real leadership. Inspiring people is not as difficult as it sounds. It starts with you — sharing with them what inspires you.

People will respond to your inspiration or vision of

what must happen, if you sound committed about what you want. If you really believe a tremendous effort is worth it, people will feel your passion. If you have doubts about the whole situation, this too will communicate itself.

> 66 The best way to inspire people to superior performance is to convince them by everything you do and by your everyday attitude that you wholeheartedly support them. 99
> (Harold Geneen, former CEO of IT&T)

Each team member's response to an appeal for a special effort depends on their deciding 'what's in it for me?' It could be respect and approval, the challenge, the kudos, the money, the chance to do what no one else has done, the joy of competing and so on.

Discover what each person and the team as a whole really wants and you have the key to unlocking their potential and sustaining that special effort.

It is your human qualities as a team leader that will attract people to consider making the supreme effort you want. For example, they will be drawn to your humanity, vulnerability, integrity and commitment. They may admire and fear your ruthless determination to make something happen, but it is the human qualities you reveal that gain people's commitment.

One team leader, for example, relies heavily on what she calls 'a well-stocked pantry'. She has an emergency supply of biscuits, sweets, and booze. When she has to call forth a special team effort, she invites everyone in and tells them the situation. Smiling broadly she says, 'Come on, let's all talk about this over some wine. See what we can come up with.'

MAKE IT APPEALING

Be creative in making a special team effort appealing:

- Can the experience become an enjoyable, competitive game?
- How could the team have fun striving for success?
- What could make the extra effort more enjoyable or worthwhile?

Advice points

When we work with sales teams a familiar complaint we often hear is that exceptional efforts to achieve a target are often rewarded by setting even higher ones. There is nothing more demotivating than the feeling that goalposts will continually be moved, no matter how hard you try. If success is punished in this way the team soon becomes demoralised.

AFTERWARDS

How you handle the aftermath of outstanding team effort will also decide whether you can call on it again one day. There has to be a definite ending to a period of exceptional team effort. Otherwise, your team may feel exploited, even confused. This is a poor recipe for seeking special help from them next time.

Nor is it sufficient merely to thank people during a quick chat in the corridor or a brief phone call. If your team has really pulled out all the stops for you, they deserve a proper thank you, in public.

CLOSURE

- Confirm that the period of exceptional effort has ended
- Acknowledge, thank and reward people
- Celebrate the team's recent efforts

Even if you cannot reward people for their recent effort with more money, find imaginative ways to convey your gratitude for what they have done. One team leader issued each person with an elaborate home-made certificate commending them for 'going far beyond the call of duty'. For years people treasured these and hung them on their office walls.

People often say they do not want official recognition because the work itself is satisfying. Even so, you lose nothing by conveying your sincere thanks for what people have done.

66 Look, I don't have to receive official recognition for anything I do. Ninety per cent of the thrill comes from knowing that the thing you designed works, and works almost the way you expected it would. **99**
(Engineer on the first 32-bit computer)

The team needs to celebrate and congratulate itself on a terrific performance, and people need to unwind and relax. Ask the team how they would like to commemorate their heroic effort.

ACTION POINTS

 Heroic effort demands creativity through constant experimentation

 Have some fun uncovering team talents

 Practise expressing vividly what is at stake

 Offer both facts and your own feelings about a request for a special effort

 Tell the team: why the special effort is essential; the exact results expected; how long any exceptional effort might be needed; the implications of succeeding; the price of failure; that you want their help

Experiment to discover what initiates and
sustains the short-lived, outstanding effort

Give attention to how you handle the aftermath
of asking for the moon

Confirm when the period of exceptional effort
will end; acknowledge, thank and reward
people; celebrate the team's recent efforts

9 How to Inspire Change in Behaviour

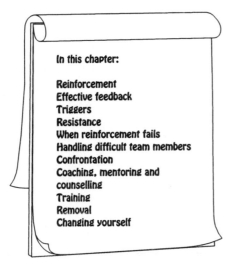

In this chapter:

Reinforcement
Effective feedback
Triggers
Resistance
When reinforcement fails
Handling difficult team members
Confrontation
Coaching, mentoring and counselling
Training
Removal
Changing yourself

'You only pay attention to me when I make mistakes.' Too many people feel this way about their working life. Inspire your team members to work more effectively by 'catching them doing things well', and telling them.

Team leaders often say, 'I'm always thinking about how well my people are doing.' Yet people cannot see inside your head. They need to hear it from you. When you do notice someone in the team doing something desirable and tell them, you are encouraging more such behaviour. This encouragement is called reinforcement.

The most obvious way that powerful leaders achieve individual change is by gaining their interest and ultimately their commitment to some goal. These leaders know they must answer the basic question a person may pose to them: 'What's in it for me?' The answer, of course, could be either a reward or a possible penalty.

Penalties or punishments are generally less effective than rewards at achieving permanent change in individuals. Yet they are commonly used by leaders who are trying to alter people's behaviour. This shows a lack of understanding about how you do in fact get what you want from people.

The three simple rules of change are:

- It is easier to change the situation than the behaviour
- It is easier to change the behaviour than the attitude
- It is easier to change the attitude than the person

Thus the hardest to alter is the person themselves, that is their personality, their beliefs and their values. Most sensible leaders do not attempt anything so fundamental and when tried it seldom works. You can, however, affect people in significant ways by indirect means so that they have to behave differently.

Thus it is relatively easy to reinforce desirable behaviour. Reinforcement works through rewarding the person in some way for behaviour *that is moving in the right direction*. No matter how small the movement, you find a way to recognise it, confirming what they did was correct and explaining how it helped. For example, if a member of a sales team achieves a small increase in monthly sales, you reinforce the desired behaviour by congratulating them (a reward), rather than complaining (punishment) that the increase should have been bigger.

Your comments have to be genuine, not manipulative. Merely being nice to someone as a way of altering behaviour seldom works.

To achieve big changes you may need to take it in stages. There might be half a dozen steps along the way to achieving the final desired behaviour. If you succeed in altering someone's behaviour once, they may still revert to the old ways. So it is important to consolidate the new behaviour before attempting to try other changes. You can only reinforce one new behaviour at a time.

ALTERING BEHAVIOUR THROUGH REINFORCEMENT

Step 1   Decide what you want the new behaviour to be

Step 2   Identify the stages needed to get there

Step 3   Watch for any sign of behaviour moving towards the first stage

Step 4   At the first sign of behaviour in the desired direction, describe to the person concerned what they did, offer encouragement and recognition; explain how this behaviour helps you or the team

Step 5   Continue reinforcing whenever the desired behaviour occurs, until it seems permanent

Step 6   Watch for signs that behaviour is moving in the desired direction of the next stage and reinforce

FEEDBACK

Someone who mistakenly thinks they are doing a great job needs to hear directly that things are not going well. Do not expect them to realise it just from hints, innuendos or vague remarks.

Telling people directly about their behaviour (feedback) is essential, since people use the information to modify their actions. So offer facts with actual examples that describe adverse performance.

Make feedback focused and not over-personalised, directing it towards specific action. Feedback that is not going to result in the recipient actually doing something may be satisfying to give but is ultimately pointless.

EFFECTIVE FEEDBACK

- Make feedback simple and memorable
- Choose a moment when the person is receptive
- Offer negative opinions in private
- Make it usable, able to lead to action
- Be specific, offer actual examples
- Avoid personal comments ('You idiot, can't you see that...')
- Check the person has really understood
- Deliver it yourself, to your own team members
- Limit it, avoid the 'and another thing' approach
- Avoid mixed messages ('It's a good report, pity it's late again')
- Give it to named people, not a general target ('Some of you are not pulling your weight' is not as good as 'Peter and Michelle, I want you both to achieve your agreed figures this month')

It takes time for people to accept a critical comment (negative feedback). Like bereavement, they may need to experience several emotional states before finally altering their behaviour. On first receiving criticism, their first reaction may be denial — 'You've got it wrong' — followed by anger — 'How dare you suggest I did that.' Rationalisation may follow — 'I had no choice, they made me do it.' Only later come their gradual acceptance and finally new behaviour. By allowing them time to absorb your comments, you enable them to find their own way to adapt to what you want.

TRIGGERS

Behaviour triggers act rather like jump leads to a car engine, helping to get it started. For example, a team member who hates rushing may immediately respond by attempting delaying tactics if you try to close a meeting too soon.

IDENTIFY THE TRIGGER

Identify the trigger to behaviour and you can:

- alter it
- eliminate it
- use it to help the person change their response

In a London design company, a team member responsible for advising on financial matters was notorious for disparaging any new ideas. Whenever anyone made a suggestion involving any expenditure, he predictably tried to kill it. The team called him Dr No.

The team explored with Dr No what was triggering this negative behaviour and came to realise that he felt his job was to ensure the company's survival. He saw any expenditure as putting that survival in jeopardy.

A combination of greater self and team awareness about this trigger enabled the team and the team member to tackle the problem.

RESISTANCE

It can be extremely frustrating to discover that some team members seem to resist altering their behaviour. Yet resistance is a normal part of the change process and you should expect it. Change is difficult for people, they may be understandably fearful about whether they can cope.

Seen from the individual team member's viewpoint, resistance often seems a perfectly sensible reaction. Once you uncover why they see the change negatively, you stand a better chance of also beginning to find ways to deal with it.

Frequently there are ways around resistance which do not require the person to change their behaviour immediately. For example, perhaps you can alter their responsibilities, making only a small adjustment rather than a big one, and so on.

WHEN REINFORCEMENT FAILS

At some time you are likely to meet the so-called 'difficult' team member. The two extreme versions of the problem person are: the high performer who is a real pain; and the troublesome performer who does not fit in.

Is the team using the person's full potential? Adverse behaviour often shows that the team is ignoring or undervaluing someone. Consider also whether the unwanted behaviour is really a symptom of a more deep-seated issue. People often have perfectly sound reasons behind apparently undesirable actions.

SOME REASONS FOR PROBLEM BEHAVIOUR

- Poor systems or methods
- Inadequate job knowledge
- Poor induction
- Lack of training
- Lack of confidence
- Medical disorders
- Stress or emotional problems
- Too much/too little responsibility
- Family difficulties
- Team pressures
- Working conditions or workload
- Cultural differences

High performers are essential to a team reaching the Success stage of its development. Teams that get on well together yet consist of mediocre performers will never be outstanding. Effective leaders somehow have to get the best from their high performers while ensuring they are properly integrated into the team.

High performers who refuse to play the team game can be a major disruption. Brilliant, individualistic, uncooperative, their success makes it hard to tackle unacceptable behaviour. For example, they may hoard information, refuse to communicate, stay out of touch for days or even weeks, and even treat colleagues with disdain. Yet their undeniable results, such as opening up

THE HIGH PERFORMER

new accounts, achieving huge orders, creating marvellous designs, often protect them from demands for change.

High performers who seem impervious to team working may undermine a whole team-based culture. People see them acting in isolation, yet being rewarded for their behaviour by highly visible signs of approval, such as pay, promotion, escaping criticism and so on. At some time you as a team leader may have to tackle an awkward high performer.

The first target for change is the high performer's reward system — both formal and informal. Can you, for example, build in extra recognition for acting as a team player? The formal reward system includes their pay, fringe benefits such as car, separate office, expense account and other perks that make life pleasant. Formal reward systems that perpetuate anti-teamwork behaviour make your life as a leader that much more difficult.

The second target for attack is the informal reward system. Look hard at whether there is implicit approval for anti-team behaviour. For example, what happens when the high performer hoards information? Do you ignore it, treat it lightly or tackle it head on?

When the high performer delivers exceptional results, do you offer unconditional approval, with no regard to how they achieved the results? If other team members see you implicitly condoning how the results were achieved, often at their expense, you will be undermining the rest of them.

Ultimately you may face a choice: obtaining the benefits of team working, or allowing one or two individuals to continue their anti-teamwork approach. Below are some actions you can take with difficult people.

THE TROUBLESOME PERFORMER This is the person who either performs badly or, despite performing adequately, makes life impossible for you or the team. Troublesome people can be anything from simply uncooperative to subtly rude or abusive, from meddlesome to excessively manipulative.

Troublesome performers underline the point that there

are really no difficult people, only unacceptable forms of behaviour.

If you hand-picked the team, it is galling when someone persists in behaving unacceptably. This can make you feel defensive, helpless, angry or embarrassed. It may even sow seeds of self-doubt. Such feelings can even prevent you sorting out the problem efficiently.

Faced with difficult behaviour you may need first to acknowledge your own feelings about it. For example, remind yourself that you do not have to respond immediately, until you have a plan. It also helps to depersonalise the behaviour by giving it a label — such as 'should listen more', 'needs to improve time keeping', 'must pick up the phone more quickly'.

Having decided to tackle the difficult behaviour, tell the person concerned how you feel and what is wrong. You can readily explain why specific behaviours like lateness, rudeness, failing to answer the phone quickly are unacceptable. Be willing to support your views with live examples.

Abstract ideas such as uncooperative, not reliable, bad attitude, inefficient, are too vague and cause misunderstandings.

---

10 TIPS FOR HANDLING DIFFICULT TEAM MEMBERS

- Discover if they are also speaking for others
- The best solutions are usually found by the whole team
- Problem people often hold the key to change
- Solve the problem, don't complain about it
- Reward good behaviour, rather than 'punishing' bad behaviour
- Analyse what triggers the adverse behaviour
- Try to identify what benefits a person obtains from their adverse behaviour
- Informally check how many others find the behaviour troublesome
- Talk about the behaviour you want, rather than complaining about behaviour you don't like

Advice points

YOUR OWN WAY

Fear often makes us reject confrontation as a way of obtaining changes in someone's behaviour. It could be fear of an unpleasant scene, of the other person's anger, or of starting something one cannot finish. Often our fear is due to our inability to handle our own emotions. Yet confrontation need not be a miserable experience. It can even be satisfying and inspiring.

Direct confrontation means tackling adverse behaviour either when it occurs, or shortly afterwards. For example, in our own team the rule is to confront someone within two weeks if they behave unacceptably. Otherwise, the issue is considered dead. This prevents resentment smouldering and gnawing away at our mutual respect and trust.

Confront by telling the truth, in a kind way. This either gets what you want, or helps the other person learn and grow. Effective confrontation starts with an 'I' statement, about what you want. Avoid indirect starts, such as 'the team feels...', 'the company would like...', 'one just does not do that sort of thing.'

Positive confrontation is saying what you want, rather than what you do not want. For example, 'I want you to get your next three reports in on time', rather than 'your next three reports must not be late.'

Although confrontation can be in public, such as during a team meeting, this may put so much pressure on the individual that they retreat into aggression, trying to defend or justify themselves. Generally, aim to have your confrontations with individuals in private.

Treat each confrontation as a voyage of discovery, where you are seeking to unravel causes, provide information and jointly agree on what must be done. Since we cannot always know the causes for a person's troublesome behaviour, it is always possible that they have a sensible reason for it. For example, they may be bad tempered because they are secretly suffering from a debilitating illness, such as constant migraines.

Confrontation

Negative

I think you're obstructive
I dislike you always being late
I consider you talk too much
I find your reports too long

Positive

I want constructive criticism
I need you to arrive on time
I want you to listen more
I need shorter reports

STEP 1	Say clearly what you want "I'd like you to listen more and be more constructive"
STEP 2	Explain clearly what effect the behaviour has on you or others "I find it insensitive when you keep interrupting"
STEP 3	Give a specific example "When John made his proposal you rushed in and rubbished it"
STEP 4	Ask for change "In our next meeting I'd like you to listen more and say how you can improve things, rather than producing negative comments"

Plan how you will tackle a private confrontation, including where it will occur. When the person arrives, greet them warmly. If you are in your own office, step out from behind your desk. Smile and say something friendly, like 'thanks... for coming. Let's both sit over here.' You will probably do this anyway, if you are an outgoing person. If you are more reserved, push yourself a little, without becoming sickly sweet.

Give some thought to the seating arrangements. Desks or tables create both a real and a psychological barrier between people. While you may feel more comfortable and protected, it will usually make the confrontation harder to handle.

If you are trying to use confrontation to persuade a team member to change, sitting next to them, side by side, makes it harder for them to be aggressive and confrontational. However, you need to be careful to allow them to retain sufficient physical space, otherwise this may make them feel intimidated.

Before the meeting, think about what the person does well. For instance: makes good sales presentations, develops leads, attends to detail. Now find some recent examples to show these in action. Even if you never use them, it reminds you that the person makes positive contributions too.

Similarly, be ready with specific examples of the behaviour you find unacceptable. Begin the meeting on a direct note by avoiding long-winded introductions or false praise. Confrontation means what it says.

Often a person knows their behaviour is causing problems. Ask if they consider that any areas in their performance need changing. If they mention the behaviour you are concerned about, use this to start negotiating the changes you want. If they do not mention it, say directly what you want. Maintain eye contact, without glaring. Wait for their reaction and if necessary ask for a response.

Use fact-seeking questions to discover whether the person sees any problems in achieving what you want. For example: 'What do you need to do it differently next time?' Adopt open-ended questions to encourage them to talk about the issue. For example: ''What do you think of your tendency to keep interrupting other team members?'

Ask the person to summarise the conversation at the end. Check that they have heard and interpreted you correctly, including the agreed action.

Permanent confrontation is tiring and no way to run a team. If your natural style thrives on confrontation, this will prevent you from obtaining the best from your team.

INSPIRING CHANGES IN BEHAVIOUR

GOODBYE TYRANNY?

Ogre leadership is on the way out. If you cannot release people's potential you probably won't reach your objective, and that has caused the downfall of the heads of some of the largest multinationals including:

- American Express
- General Motors
- Kodak
- Digital Equipment
- IBM

Talking point

Coaching is personal help given to develop skills and improve a person's way of working. It is a highly practical activity concerned with today's tasks, not a future job. It is an art and best learned by practice.

COACHING

66In the future, the ability of an organisation to give proper attention to the needs of the individual will be critical, and the most effective means of delivering this will be by building coaching into daily life, and developing it as an activity alongside leading and managing. 99
(Geoff Keeys,
Director of Personnel and Business Services, Prudential Corporation)

When the issue is unacceptable team behaviour you cannot easily pass responsibility for coaching to someone else. Coaching is likely to involve an ongoing relationship in which you act as a partner and catalyst. A sign of a successful coaching session is when the other person feels the conversation is between two equals, one of whom has more knowledge or expertise.

Coaching can enhance your own skill as a leader. You learn to respond to the other person's needs, while tailoring their personal development to the organisation's needs as well as their own.

The essence of coaching is establishing the person's current behaviour, agreeing learning'objectives and then creating live opportunities for them to practise the new behaviour. You also create opportunities for feedback and further development.

66We simply cannot afford the luxury of managing people in the same way as we have in the past. All managers have had to become more of a coach and counsellor, leaders who are receptive to the notion of empowerment. 99
(Stephen Croni,
Group Personnel Director, Rank Xerox)

MENTORING

Another way of tackling difficult behaviour is by linking the person with someone they respect, who acts like an adviser.

The mentor may be another team member, someone in a different part of the organisation or even outside it. The mentor is a source of wisdom, advice and support, not a person in authority. Finding the right one can be tricky. Ask the team member if they have someone in mind. The mentor must be properly briefed, either by you or the team member. You will then have to leave it to the mentor to find a way forward.

COUNSELLING

Counselling is a rather indirect way of inspiring changed behaviour. It is usually better to use the services of an independent trained counsellor from outside the organisation. Professional counsellors do not coach but work primarily through people's feelings and emotions.

You can use counselling if the problem seems to touch on a person's strong emotions and feelings. The person must be willing to accept such help. You cannot enforce counselling, except as a condition for continued employment. For some work-related problems it can also work surprisingly quickly. Three or four sessions may be enough to enable someone to begin developing different behaviour. However, for more fundamental issues the person may need a more in-depth approach such as personal therapy.

Off-the-job training is yet another way of inspiring changed team member behaviour, if the issue is essentially concerned with a specific skill. For example, if someone rambles excessively, constantly talking in team meetings, or is over-aggressive, perhaps they would benefit from some presentation or communication training. If the person seems disorganised, maybe time management training would help.

Where possible, discuss the proposed solution with both the individual concerned and a specialist adviser. The latter can suggest whether training as a solution is likely to work and how long it might take.

Training should bring results within a clear timetable. However, you are part of the formula for success and must develop a plan for supporting the person before and after they experience training. Support involves explaining the need for the training, how it might benefit them, and their prospects. You also confirm your intention to help them apply their new learning within the team.

After the training you take responsibility for checking that the person has opportunities for applying their new skills, and encouraging them when they do.

SOME WAYS TO INFLUENCE BEHAVIOUR

Orders. For people needing exact instructions and where compliance is essential. 'Do it now.' 'It must be done this way.'

Requests. For people who like to be asked. 'I have a difficulty.' 'Next time could you...?'

Advice. For people who prefer guidance or are influenced by the logic of the situation. 'You might try...' 'The drawback of that is...'

Criticism. For people who respond to negative feedback. 'What you did wrong was...' 'Why on earth did you...?'

Promises. For people who find the task unattractive or need extra motivation. '... then I'll give you...' 'If you succeed we will...'

Explanations. For people who are motivated by understanding the reasons for doing something. '... because...' 'The reason is that...'

Threats. For people who do not respond to more positive methods, and where compliance is essential. 'If you don't....' 'Do as I say or I'll...'

Leading questions. For people who respond to a signal or need to overcome their reticence. 'You must agree that ...' 'Don't you think that...?'

Praise. For everyone, especially those who respond to immediate feedback. 'That was excellent because...' 'Well done.'

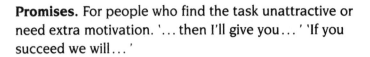

THE IMPOSSIBLE TEAM MEMBER

If you have tried all the above, what next? Occasionally you meet a team member who seems almost impossible to work with. No matter what you do, the person fails to respond. You keep doing all the right things, yet still the person is still obstructive, or seemingly resistant to any suggestions.

There are no impossible people, only impossible behaviours. This is an important distinction. Once you write off a person as 'impossible', you leave no real avenues for achieving change. The only real solution is to part company.

Behind every impossible behaviour there is always a reason. It may not be worth the effort to try to uncover it. The alternative is not to bother, instead focusing only on the form of new behaviour you want, and dealing specifically with divergences from it.

Once you have concluded there is no further justification in trying to alter the person's team behaviour you have two remaining choices: either to neutralise the person within the team, or to arrange their removal from it.

Try neutralising them first. Rather than tackling the person's actual behaviour, devise ways to reduce or eliminate its impact. For instance, suppose a team member repeatedly argues with team decisions. Rather than trying to stop them each time, find a way of making decisions differently, such as a decision-making procedure that reduces their opportunity to argue.

Or suppose someone keeps complaining about the team agenda, the minutes, the organisation of the meeting, how long it takes, and so on. You might give them responsibility for constructing the agenda or taking the minutes, perhaps even chairing the meeting for certain items.

REMOVAL

Even if you want to remove someone from your team, often you cannot because you lack sufficient authority, time, or need their special expertise. Even if you succeed in removing someone you could have an unpleasant surprise. Once they have gone, someone else often emerges to cause a new set of behaviour problems. Removal is therefore always a last resort.

If removal also means the person losing their job you will need powerful reasons for your action: grounds such as dishonesty, absenteeism, substance abuse, sexual harassment, low productivity. It usually pays to discuss the removal of someone from your team with an adviser experienced in this area. People are more protected these days by anti-discrimination legislation and employment guidelines.

It is worth consulting any company guidelines on dismissal. Company policy and employment law must be considered before embarking on this final course of action.

CHANGE YOURSELF

Although it is common to see difficulties with a team member as the other person's fault, problems are often based around relationships. For example, is the person a thorn in everyone's side, or just yours? While the focus in this chapter has been on altering the behaviour of others, it is often easier and quicker to adjust your own. If you are 50 per cent responsible for a relationship not working, then first try to change your own side of the equation. Doing this may produce a change in the other person too.

ACTION POINTS

 Try to catch people doing things well and tell them

 Use reinforcement to guide changes in difficult behaviour

 Try to identify what triggers the unacceptable behaviour

 Be highly specific about what is unacceptable behaviour — give examples

 Confront over adverse behaviour by telling the truth, in a kind or supportive way

 Tell the person what behaviour you want to see, rather than what you don't want to see

 Start confrontations with 'I' statements

 Treat confrontation as a voyage of discovery

 If you decide to confront, do it sooner rather than later

If you decide to confront, do it sooner rather than later

 As a last resort, neutralise adverse behaviour or arrange removal of the person from the team

 Consider whether it is also appropriate to alter your own behaviour

10 How to Encourage Inter-team Working

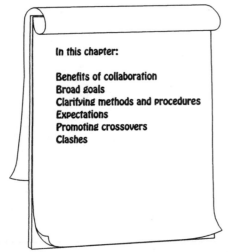

In this chapter:

Benefits of collaboration
Broad goals
Clarifying methods and procedures
Expectations
Promoting crossovers
Clashes

The gates open and the empty shell of a newly painted LandRover Discovery glides onto the waiting platform. Moments later the platform rises dramatically 20 feet, to align precisely with the start of the production track. Over the next few hours the shell is steadily transformed until, gleaming and pristine, it is driven away ready for sale.

Scores of separate LandRover production teams must do their tasks so others further down the track can complete theirs. Only if everyone acts as expected does the production line run smoothly. Inevitably, problems arise. This is when the real test of team working surfaces. How the teams relate to each other, solving difficulties together, is an important influence on the success of the company's entire production process.

Inter-team working occurs in many different ways. A company may establish cross-functional teams, or an existing team may need to start relating to another, perhaps outside the organisation. Two internal teams may face a common challenge and requirement to cooperate, and so on.

You probably have little or no direct control over other people's teams. Yet you may need to support inter-team work. This is increasingly a concern of organisations that rely heavily on teams to produce outstanding results. Promoting inter-team work can prove puzzling and intractable. While there are no instant solutions, you can encourage the process in various practical ways.

BENEFITS OF COLLABORATION

Despite the obvious difficulties, there are considerable advantages to be gained from different teams collaborating across organisational, national and international boundaries. The mixture of cultures, education and experience can generate important new solutions and viewpoints. The teams may see opportunities that one team working alone would miss.

Even within a single organisation there are benefits from one or more teams working together, for example the ability to offer customers a better service. In the international insurance brokers Sedgwicks, for instance, there were two teams with different responsibilities. Each would occasionally find customers unsuitable for their particular service yet wholly suitable for the other. But because the teams acted competitively they never passed on these clients' names. This worked to the detriment of both the customers and the whole company. With outside help the two teams discovered an acceptable way to deal with their competitiveness and still work together. They went further and realised the mutual benefits of shared information.

The mixture of skills is yet another reason for

encouraging good inter-team working, since many problems can be tackled using a wider range of abilities. For instance, a financial auditing team working collaboratively with a production department may jointly find better ways of arranging deliveries of raw materials or reducing stock levels.

BROAD GOALS

You can inspire successful inter-team working through ensuring that there is a broad inter-team goal. This should be one that extends beyond the boundaries of either team to create a unifying factor. Try to establish it by both teams working together to define it. Such goals are often extremely challenging, requiring entirely new ways of working.

Some well-established teams possess such a strong identity and clear focus that the only way they can collaborate with other powerful teams is through choosing an entirely new, broad goal. This means creating a fresh agenda on which both can concentrate. For example, what do both teams really want to achieve, what are the priorities, who establishes these, and how long will the joint working arrangements last?

You cannot take it for granted that people in two teams that must work together automatically understand the benefits. For example, where a company team has to work closely with one from a competitor, the members may first need careful convincing about the advantages of such an arrangement that may anyway be short lived.

Two high-tech British companies agreed to bid for a major defence contract. Their two teams, however, failed to sort out who was leading the attempt. They entered the formal presentation without ever resolving this important issue.

The customer's own panel judging the bids was headed by a fiery, no-nonsense Air Force commander. After listening for a while to the two teams giving their presentations, he finally exploded: 'For heavens sake, which of you is heading this proposal? Can't you two get your act together?' Not surprisingly, the two teams did not win the contract.

METHODS

It will almost certainly make sense to help the various teams clarify their respective roles. For instance, who does what, and is there a single leader or coordinator? It also makes sense to nail down procedures that each will use during their collaboration. For example, how will the teams monitor and report joint progress and what mechanisms will they use to resolve inter-team conflicts? Also, are there procedures for recruiting new team members and so on?

EXPECTATIONS

Whoever is sponsoring the inter-team working has to clarify expectations about the new arrangements. Expectations may be frustrated if they conflict with entrenched team views about not cooperating with another team. Sponsors can include a board of directors, a head of department, a customer and even shareholders.

It is also essential that sponsors stay committed to this new arrangement. The teams will require time to build links and explore across their respective boundaries. During this difficult process, whoever initiates the inter-team approach should stay available to offer encouragement and troubleshoot.

The head of an large IT department wanted his project managers to work together more closely. Until then, project managers and their teams had been encouraged to work in isolation, competing on performance, seldom communicating and never sharing ideas or resources.

All the teams greeted the new demand with great scepticism. Their reactions proved justified. Faced with the difficulties of undoing a history of rivalry, the IT manager eventually abandoned his expectations for joint working.

If you are responsible for encouraging inter-team working, avoid talking too much in generalities and get down to specifics. For example, do both sets of people agree they should meet weekly? Build agreement across the teams about the regularity of progress reporting. This needs to be done in depth and the results reviewed carefully.

Inter-team working demands regular joint decision making. This takes time, particularly if the teams come from different national cultures. Be patient with the consensus building that must occur to achieve commitment. By allowing enough time to resolve problems early in relationships, you help the teams develop maturity for making hard joint decisions later.

PROMOTE CROSSOVERS

Begin reducing the barriers between teams by giving members insights into each other's way of working. For example, arrange for team members to shadow each other's jobs for a day. Or negotiate that members of one team should work for a while in the other team, perhaps working on a common problem or challenge.

Another approach is to ask a couple of team members to visit the other team and report back on any lessons they see for joint working. Many problems of inter-team working stem simply from a lack of understanding about the other team.

However, it is seldom sensible to ask a team member to join another team for a prolonged period just to promote better joint working. The individual concerned may 'turn native', with prolonged contact with the host team weakening their loyalty to the original team.

FOCUS ON CLASHES

Clashes between teams often arise because of genuine cultural differences — national, racial or organisational. While not necessarily insurmountable, they do require significant time and effort to sort them out. For example, a team used to working in a non-hierarchical way may find it hard to relate to one enmeshed in a bureaucratic structure.

A consultancy team with a simple reporting structure may find it hard to understand their opposite numbers in a local government department with several layers of management to appease. Similarly, the local government team may find it threatening or undermining to deal with a team that seems to have little respect for hierarchy.

Whatever the issue, inter-team working makes heavy demands on team leaders to oil the wheels and resolve conflicts. It is important to acknowledge these conflicts and not gloss over them.

ACTION POINTS

 You can encourage inter-team working in many different ways

 Identify a broad inter-team goal, extending beyond the boundaries of either team

 Establish inter-team goals through both teams working together

☑ Help team members understand the benefits of working across mutual boundaries

☑ Clarify who is sponsoring the inter-team working

☑ Whoever promotes inter-team working needs to stay committed to this arrangement

☑ Initiators of inter-team working should stay around to offer encouragement, troubleshoot and push for change

☑ Clarify the mutual expectations of the two teams and get down to specifics

☑ Clarify the methods and procedures the teams will use to work together

☑ Build agreement across the teams about the regularity of progress reporting

☑ Avoid stating rigid ground rules for inter-team working, since expectations will alter over time

☑ Inter-team working demands regular joint decision making, which takes time

☑ Reduce barriers by giving team members insights into each other's way of working

☑ Acknowledge the conflicts

☑ Inter-team clashes require significant time and effort to address them effectively

How to be an Adaptable Leader 11

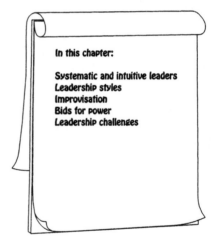

In this chapter:

Systematic and intuitive leaders
Leadership styles
Improvisation
Bids for power
Leadership challenges

Indecisive, unable to delegate and occasionally rescued from complete chaos by his wife. This is how best-selling author Bob Woodward of the *Washington Post* described Bill Clinton in his 1994 inside look at the president's administration. Virtually all members of his inner circle, including Mrs Clinton, Woodward found, 'were critical of the President's management style.'

What did they mean by his style? That like President Johnson he swore crudely, or that like Nixon he constantly lied? Did he spend too much time playing golf like Eisenhower, or have no real idea what he wanted to achieve like Bush? When they talked of style, did they really mean Clinton's personality?

People often confuse style with personality. They are not quite the same. You can more readily adapt your style than alter your basic personality. Personality is a complex brew of traits, habits, personal expression and emotional make-up, created over many years. Leadership style is rather simpler. It is about how you behave *as a leader*, relating to people and influencing your team. There is no definite right or wrong way, since teams and circumstances vary. What works well for you can fail miserably if tried by someone else.

Having a choice of how to lead greatly expands your ability to respond appropriately to different situations. Rather than trying to alter your personality, you adapt your leadership behaviour so that others want to follow your direction.

How adaptable you are as a leader may well determine your own and the team's success. For example, some senior managers start every new job convinced that the best step is immediately to restructure their department or area of influence. They do this simply because it produced good results in the past. Yet this may not suit the new situation. Thus adapting your style may well consist of *not* doing something you did previously.

Similarly, if you are someone who relies on always approaching situations in a systematic way, there may be occasions when it is more appropriate to rely on your intuition. Finding the right balance between being systematic and intuitive is another example of how effective leaders adapt their style.

WHEN FORMAL MEETS INFORMAL

Teams that cross organisational boundaries are often created for powerful commercial reasons, such as to make bids for major contracts. Such teams bring into sharp focus a difference between adaptive and non-adaptive leadership behaviour.

A fast growing, US-based computer servicing corporation briefly joined forces with IBM to bid for one of the world's largest outsourcing contracts. The clash of informal versus formal leadership styles prevented a true partnership.

For example, the servicing company's people expected their chief executive to attend really important mega-bids of the kind they now faced. The CEO and his senior colleagues were highly adaptable and would drop whatever they were doing if they thought they could help clinch the deal. These same servicing people also requested the attendance of IBM's chief executive. Despite the huge stakes, he delegated the task to another board member.

Also, the locally based IBM team members were in considerable awe of their senior executives. The latter expected and received excessive deference to their views. This prevented important issues from being thoroughly thrashed out before the final bid presentation.

Similarly, the computer servicing people were familiar with their own company's delegating style of leadership. This left them free to take large decisions without constantly referring up the hierarchy. By contrast, the IBMers were more comfortable with referring anything contentious up the chain of command.

These two incompatible styles made it hard to build a temporary cross-organisational arrangement that worked well. Ultimately the bid by the two teams failed.

SYSTEMATIC LEADERS

- Make choices using a logical sequence of steps
- Justify decisions by evidence
- Identify constraints
- Emphasise the need for information
- Hate relying on guesses or gut reaction

INTUITIVE LEADERS

- Jump from one logical step to another, then back again
- Avoid specifics while visualising the total situation
- Continuously redefine problems
- Justify decisions by results
- Rapidly explore and drop alternatives
- Follow instinct, often act impulsively

66 I do not believe in a management style where you point and say 'Go that way.' But if you say 'I'm going this way, please come with along with me,' you can achieve a great deal. **99** (Steve Shirley, chair of the 1000-employee £25 million turnover FI Group plc)

Adaptability is something you can work on, it is not a fixed quantity. It means exercising important muscles your already have: seeing what is required; using your repertoire of responses; improvising.

SEEING

The ability to see what is happening in the moment, to realise what the situation requires, sets leaders apart from managers, distinguishes inspiring leaders from pedestrian ones, and contributes to that ill-defined and intangible factor, charisma.

In order to *see*, you must be willing to keep looking again at what is happening in the team. You keep trying to answer for yourself the basic question: 'What is happening at this moment?'

For example, you look to see how team members are relating to each, the nature and quality of their interactions. You check out the communication that is occurring — are people, for instance, saying what they mean, and meaning what they say?

You look to see what will inspire and energise people, which may be different in the morning to what they require in the afternoon. You can only find the answer to what kind of direction and support to offer through seeing.

You look to see what will get your message across in the most effective way, picking up clues from what is happening and what other people are saying. When you are really looking in this way, you will begin to sense what each situation needs. For example, how mature is the team? Or putting this question slightly differently, where is the team on the development clock we showed in Chapter 6?

You gain practice in seeing by doing the leadership job. You can also expand your capacity to see through learning to understand team processes, how people are working together and interacting. There are, for example, specialist workshops where you can practise the art of seeing what is happening and learn to interpret the implication in terms of your own leadership action.

REPERTOIRE

You do not see a parrot smiling, nor a snake grinning. Most animals have an extremely limited range of expression, unlike human beings. We are able to respond with a huge range of expressions. This is part of what separates us from other animals.

Effective leaders also need to develop their repertoire both of expressions and their responses to team situations. Yet how do you expand your repertoire? The main way is through trying different approaches and seeing the effect they have. Another important way is through working on your own personal development — your growth as a human being. If we want a plant to grow strong and healthy, we can either let nature take its course, or give it a little help by adding some plant food.

Similarly, you do not need merely to let nature take its course in your personal development. Through avenues such as training, coaching, mentoring, and self-development workshops, you can deliberately seek to enhance your personal growth. When people are interested in their own personal growth they naturally expand their repertoire of responses.

ADAPTING TO THE SITUATION   Two areas where as a leader you can use your adaptability to good effect lie in the amount of *direction* and *support* you offer the team. You vary these to match the team and its task. How exactly do you do this?

First, you focus direction by helping people understand what they are supposed to do, bringing clarity to tasks. You summarise regularly, so people know where they are heading. Secondly, you offer support by promoting two-way communication. You do this through active listening, encouragement, dealing with tension or conflict, and helping people solve problems.

Assuming you are willing to adapt your leadership style to offer varying amounts of direction and support, how do you choose what is required at any one moment? The most important factor again is seeing — seeing what the team needs, seeing what individuals require, seeing what is happening at any one moment.

USING THE REPERTOIRE

A newly appointed general manager of a division of a major car company in Britain discovered that Peter, one member of the team he had inherited, engaged in highly divisive tactics and office 'politics'.

Shortly after helping the team agree an important new policy, the general manager sat in a widely attended meeting only to hear Peter giving his own, totally different summary of the team's policy.

The general manager flatly contradicted Peter's summary of the policy, insisting he either state the correct one, or let someone else do it for him.

After the meeting, one of the General Manager's senior colleagues commented, 'Weren't you a bit hard on Peter in that meeting, after all he's on your team?'

'No,' replied the general manager. 'I knew that taking him aside afterwards would do no good. I needed to give a clear and public message that I want people to stick to agreed team policies.'

Later the general manager called Peter to his office and reinforced his public message by spelling out the consequences of such behaviour in the future. 'If you deliberately do it again, you won't be an employee of this company.'

The general manager used two different responses to the situation, rather than just one. His repertoire has expanded over the years, as he himself admits. 'When I consider how I responded in the past to certain situations, I realise my repertoire has grown, since I did not act appropriately to them.'

A mature team requires less direction and support than an immature one. Maturity in this sense is not chronological age, but stage of development. Four common styles that show how you could differ in offering direction and support are delegating, participating, selling and telling.

Delegating

You adopt a *delegating* style by allowing team members to 'get on with it'. You intervene very little, either to direct or engage in two-way discussions. If your team is quite mature, needing only small amounts of direction and support, this might be an appropriate way of leading. Suppose your team has been together for some time and there is strong mutual trust, with people clear about both direction and what has to be done. In this situation it would make sense to give as much responsibility to other people as possible.

Participating

You use a *participating* style by not giving orders. Instead, you hold frequent conversations with your team, so people can agree on what needs doing and how to do it. Suppose your team is well used to working together, yet is now facing major new challenges. To respond well to these probably means using everyone's ideas. So it is sensible to involve them in deciding how to tackle the challenges, letting them influence important choices.

Selling

A *selling* style means you are directive, yet also engage in frequent discussion. You encourage a two-way conversation with team members. This is a style for a moderately immature team requiring plenty of support and direction. Suppose your team is quite young, inexperienced and unsure of itself. You may see a need to be more assertive about how you want things to be, and to convince them that your requirements are in their best interests.

Telling

With a *telling* style you give considerable direction and instruction. You seldom invite much discussion or ask for feedback. This approach may initially help an immature team that demands mainly direction though not much support. Suppose your team is used to receiving orders and then carrying them out without much argument. This team will probably not bother much with the bigger picture, simply doing as directed. In that situation, your leadership behaviour is to make your requests unambiguous and straightforward through the telling style.

FOUR COMMON LEADERSHIP STYLES

- Delegating
- − Not much direction
- − Not much support
- Participating
- − Some direction
- − Plenty of support
- Selling
- − A fair amount of direction
- − Much support
- Telling
- − Much direction
- − Not much support

These four forms of leadership behaviour are merely descriptions, they do not explain either how you can adopt them or whether they are entirely appropriate to your team. Their essential message is the need to *see* what the team needs and adapt to the situation.

They are also a useful framework for reviewing your style. For example, if you find yourself constantly *telling* your team what to do, is it time to explore ways to help it become more mature and able to take more initiatives? People may seem comfortable just accepting orders, yet this will tend to drain your own energies and it will not be utilising people's creative talents.

IMPROVISATION

It is all very well seeing what is needed, or even having the right ability to respond in your repertoire, but can you actually perform when the situation demands it? To be a successful team leader you also have to improvise.

Improvisation is producing a response without prolonged planning, often instinctively. The best actors do it on stage when they forget their lines — good leaders do it even more often.

Improvisation is not nearly as difficult as it can seem from watching someone else doing it. It comes with practice, and stems from being open to tackling situations in a creative, unexpected way, rather than always relying on what you did in the past.

"If you do what you've always done, you get what you've always got. **"**

When leaders improvise they are seeing what is needed, scanning their repertoire of responses and then making something up that seems appropriate. In doing so they also further expand their repertoire.

When we run management workshop exercises we often use theatre improvisation exercises. The leaders and managers who take part are frequently impressed by their own ability to find new sources of creativity and inspiration. They soon realise that in their own field they can improvise just as well as any stand-up comedian. Developing your ability to improvise includes building your self-confidence, learning to tap into your creativity, and taking risks.

The ideal style

There have been many attempts to define the ideal leadership style. People have looked at successful leaders, tried to analyse how they do it and then suggested the rest of us should do the same. This does not work. Your success as a leader will depend on your personality, your style, and what your particular team needs.

Some companies have tried articulating the sort of leaders they want by listing characteristics they want to observe in action. Federal Express, for instance, expects: charisma, concern for the individual, intellectual stimulation, courage, dependability, flexibility, integrity, judgement, and respect for others.

These are useful guides, yet there have been many successful leaders who did not seem to exhibit these desirable traits. For instance, not all effective leaders have proved totally dependable, and others have shown scant concern for the individual. However, you could argue that they succeeded despite these drawbacks.

W H SMITH — GROUP STYLE OF LEADERSHIP

Managers develop a style which:

- Emphasises directness, openness to ideas, commitment to the success of others, a willingness to accept personal accountability and the strong development of teamwork and trust. Differing views will be sought, values and honesty encouraged, not suppressed.
- Follows clear and well-understood decision-making processes.
- Is clear about Group, team and individual performance goals. People must have a clear understanding of their responsibilities and their performance targets.
- Makes full use of the skills and abilities of people and provides excellent training and development opportunities.
- Gives recognition to individuals and teams who contribute to our success. Recognition must be given to individuals who contribute; to those who create and innovate, as well as those who support the day-to-day business.
- Gives an honest and regular appraisal of their performance and career prospects.
- Sets high standards of integrity.
- Increases the authority and responsibility of those who are closest to our products and our customers. By actively pushing responsibility, trust and recognition throughout the organisation, we can release and benefit from the full capabilities of our people.

Source: Internal company document

BIDS FOR POWER

If you are new to leading a team, you may be wondering 'How do I manage to stay in charge?' Though it is an understandable concern, it is really the wrong question. The real challenge is: 'How can I unlock my team's full potential?'

The informal use of power on the part of other team

members can occasionally threaten your formal role. For example, if one or more team members start to abuse their informal leadership positions, it may affect your own ability to make things happen and get things done.

Again, what matters is seeing and responding appropriately from your repertoire. Generally informal leadership within the team is a sign of success and it is best to welcome it as an ally.

MAKING SENSE OF LEADERSHIP CHALLENGES

It can be hard to distinguish between attempts to subvert your formal role and genuine contributions from people wanting to get things done.

Inexperienced team leaders may see constant threats whenever team members challenge:

- work priorities
- what should be discussed
- the acceptability of decisions
- the direction in which the team is going
- what each person should do
- the use of resources

These challenges are not always concerned with who is leading. Often they are genuine attempts to become clearer about what needs to be done.

ACTION POINTS

 Adapt your leadership behaviour rather than trying to alter your personality

 To enhance your adaptability keep developing: your ability to see what is required; your repertoire of responses; your ability to improvise

 Assume that informal leadership will regularly move around the team

Tailor the amount of direction and support you give to the nature of the team and the task

 Allow the maturity of your team's development to influence how you adapt your leadership style

 Avoid relying solely on formal power to get things done

 By responding positively to team challenges you demonstrate an adaptable leadership style

 Power is not a fixed quantity — cultivate it

 By adopting an empowering leadership style, you help release people's personal or informal power

12 How to Harness a Team's Power

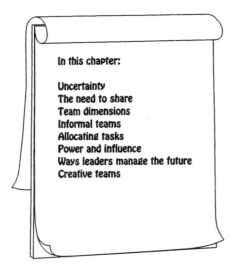

You do not need an orchestra to whistle a tune. Equally, it takes an orchestra to play a symphony. Certain tasks may look suitable for the team to undertake yet turn out later not to be. With so much emphasis on teams in organisations, you may be tempted to believe they can handle just about anything. What then is *not* suitable for a team?

As a team leader, policy maker, trainer or developer, you will face many situations requiring the completion of an important task. Part of being an adaptable leader is showing flexibility in choosing the best solutions for getting it done. One misconception is that teams always outsmart the individual. This is certainly untrue. Often the best solution is to pass a task to an individual rather than the team.

In senior management groups, for instance, far too much time tends to be wasted on trying to pretend they are a team. Either such a group is far too big and unwieldy to act in unison, or there is too much interpersonal competition and clashing egos. Also, in such teams fairly basic operational issues often dominate. Since up to 90 per cent of a senior manager's time is spent on mainly functional or operational matters, team working is not always a sensible solution.

How do you judge whether tasks are best done by a team or an individual? Two useful criteria are *uncertainty* and the *need to share*.

UNCERTAINTY

If there is not a great deal of uncertainty about the task to be done, then teamwork may not be appropriate. For example, suppose an office of four people needs a new phone system. A single individual could probably sort out the best solution and get it installed rather than all four people trying to act as a team to do it. This does not mean the individual ignores the other three, only that after hearing their views completing the task is probably more easily and quickly done alone.

A task such as planning and choosing a strategic direction is more complex. There are many unknowns and probably no one individual can think through all the implications thoroughly.

Talking point

EXAMPLES OF PROBLEMS THAT IMPLY GREAT UNCERTAINTY AND NEED A TEAM APPROACH

- For ICI: How do we deal with a hostile takeover bid?
- For CSC: How do we bid successfully for the world's largest outsourcing contracts?
- For BP: How do we change our corporate culture?
- For Sainsbury's: How do we deal with increasing competition in our market?
- For Burton Group: How do we move from mainly full-time staff to mainly part-timers?

There are scaled down versions of these for any departmental or sectional team. In each case team members come to the table equally unsure, or lacking the full picture.

NEED TO SHARE

If the task requires the collective skills, wisdom or knowledge of several people, teamwork is ideal. For example, the only way to achieve total quality is by engaging everyone in the organisation. Production, design engineering, marketing and sales all need to work closely together. Only through teamwork can they combine to improve radically products and services.

Conversely, where the task does not need all or even some of the other team members, it is probably best handled by an individual. It may require consultation with others, yet not demand their active involvement.

Advice points

The practical conclusions from this are: select tasks for the team that involve a great deal of uncertainty; select tasks for the team that require people to share in order to handle them.

TEAM DIMENSIONS

When people talk about teams, they often refer to the formal ones that have been established within the organisational structure. These are the project groups, divisional or sectional teams, the executive board and so on. But formalised teams are not the only ones around. In most organisations there are informal teams. These are not necessarily tightly controlled or required to focus on particular results. They are loose groupings of sectional interests, bringing together like-minded people who enjoy being with each other.

These informal teams satisfy people's need for belonging, self-esteem and recognition. Without detailed terms of reference, these unofficial teams nevertheless generate high levels of commitment, motivation and creativity. Many tasks are best handled through them since they are less constrained by rules and procedures. You do not attempt to 'manage' or control such teams. It is better to hand them a problem and trust them to produce some answers. Nor can you readily discipline such a casual grouping, since they are not directly accountable to you.

Another dimension to consider is the life of your team. In an increasing number of organisations teams are rapidly assembled, do a specific job and then disperse. New ones are created as required. This is how Sun Microsystems, for instance, has grown into a global company. Its whole philosophy is to keep creating new teams to tackle new issues. Often you may have the opportunity of creating teams within teams. You ask a few people to tackle a problem and soon they begin acting as a separate team.

> The practical conclusions from this are: select tasks for informal groups that use their creative flair, their commitment to what they like doing together, and their informality in circumventing formal rules and procedures. In creating sub-teams set clear time limits for their existence and insist these are honoured.

Advice points

TIME CONSTRAINTS

Through sheer weight of numbers, teams can work amazingly quickly. Yet a single person acting with total dedication can often do just as well or better. In many cases there are 'too many cooks', with team members getting in each other's way, rather than complementing each other.

If there is a lot at stake and time is short, a single person's judgement may ultimately be the best response. For example, a project team may labour to make sense of the implications of a major new investment opportunity, yet the final decision whether or not to proceed might best be made by one person.

Advice points

> The practical conclusions from this are: consider giving long-term tasks to teams, short-term tasks to individuals; consider giving complex tasks to teams and simple tasks to individuals.

THE TEAM MEETING

During team meetings many issues may arise that potentially could involve everyone. It can be tempting to do just that. On closer inspection though, some matters may be clearly inside one member's own specialist area of work. Others may need to know what is happening without necessarily becoming involved in the work. It is part of your developing leadership skill to analyse which issues are narrow ones, suitable for the involvement of a single person, and which justify a more collective approach.

In a group struggling to establish itself as a coherent team, everyone may feel they have an obligation to become involved in everyone else's business. Watch out for this excessive form of team involvement where a more appropriate response may be quickly to delegate the matter to just one or two people. The rest of the team are then literally minding their own business.

In our own company, for example, we introduced regular project management meetings to track the progress of large contracts with clients. Initially we expected the whole team to be present. It soon became clear that only the relevant project manager and the person dealing directly with the client really needed to be there.

> The practical conclusion from this is: in team meetings select carefully issues that need to involve everyone and deal promptly with items that can be simply delegated to an individual.

Advice points

POWER AND INFLUENCE

When an actor comes on stage playing a king, he only looks king-like if the other cast members behave as if he has authority. In essence, they give up some of their own performance power to enable the king to seem kingly.

Similarly in organisations, formal power may initially come from your official role or title. Yet you will only seem 'leader-like' if people choose to treat you as a leader. People enable leaders to have power. Followers therefore make leadership possible, by relinquishing some of their own power.

Power is your own ability to get things done and it depends on both formal and informal sources of authority. You never hold absolute authority. You always face restrictions imposed by your organisation or the situation. Using formal power to obtain what you want means relying on the hierarchy or on hard-to-challenge sources such as laws and regulations — for example, health and safety requirements.

for example: by building lists of of people who can help you and the team

Use political & networking skills

 for example: by encouraging away days and constantly refreshing yourself with new stimuli

Take an overview, stand back from the day-to-day

 for example: by knowing your priorities and sticking to them

Focus your time & energy

for example: by constantly testing how much responsibility you can pass on to team members

Encourage shared power

 for example: by analysing team work methods

Develop ways to learn what is happening

for example: by adopting different approaches to team issues

Alter your approach to match circumstances

 for example: by being an excellent listener, discovering what people need

Respond sensitively to needs of team members

 for example: by encouraging other team members to participate in making important choices

Avoid monopolising decision making

 for example: by identifying who will do what

Help clarify people's roles

for example: by speaking up for your team in the right circles

Represent your team in the corridors of power

 for example: by spending time on clarifying purpose and expectations

Focus attention on defining clear objectives and establishing standards

 for example: by expecting the team to ask questions, such as "why do we do it that way?"

Question fixed rules or ways of working

Increasing your leadership influence

LEADERS RELYING ON FORMAL POWER

- Demand absolute respect for the leader
- Insist on unquestioning obedience or compliance
- Expect all decisions to be unchallenged
- Prefer to control rather than empower

LEADERS RELYING ON INFORMAL POWER

- Expect to have to earn respect
- Know they must win compliance
- Expect some decisions to be open to challenge
- Prefer to empower rather than control

Those who rely mainly on formal power to get things done tend to be weaker leaders than those who rely mainly on their informal power. For example, in some branches of catering the leadership remains strictly hierarchical. Yet it is becoming increasingly unrealistic to expect such behaviour from today's teams. One reason is the formation of teams that do not owe any strong allegiance to the leader, such as inter-departmental project teams or cross-organisation teams.

Formal power based on your official leadership title is seldom enough to create a successful team. You also need to:

- offer reward through praise
- punish by disapproval
- influence through relationships
- share knowledge with personal contacts
- initiate through ideas
- achieve change through taking personal responsibility

However, other team members can also do these to obtain what they want. When they do that they are exercising informal leadership. How should you react to such challenging behaviour? By welcoming informal leadership you are showing you have an adaptable leadership style.

Talking point

10 WAYS LEADERS MANAGE THE FUTURE

- *They manage the dream* — create a compelling vision, define reality
- *They embrace error* — are not afraid of making mistakes and admit them when they do
- *They encourage reflective talkback* — welcome personal feedback about themselves
- *They encourage dissent* — encourage contrary views and those who can distinguish between the expected and what is happening
- *They possess the Nobel factor* — exude optimism, faith and hope
- *They understand the Pygmalion effect* — expect the best from people around them, stretching them without letting them fall too short, too often
- *They have and use instinct* — possess a sense of where the culture is going to be, where the team must be if it is to grow
- *They see the long view* — have patience
- *They understand stakeholder symmetry* — know they must reconcile competing claims of interested parties
- *They create strategic alliances and partnerships* — see the world globally, knowing there is now nowhere to hide

Source: Adapted from *On Becoming a Leader*, Warren Bennis (Hutchinson Books, 1989)

Power is not a fixed quantity. It grows according to relationships with followers. It dies when people will no longer follow, when they take back their power.

Since you cannot monopolise power, you must expect the informal leadership role to move around, from member to member. People increasingly recognise the importance of this phenomenon, now often called empowerment.

Empowerment is a challenge to those who think the only effective leadership style is through exercising strong, formal power. With an empowering leadership approach, you deliberately try to release other people's personal or informal sources of power. You do so by not relying unduly on your formal authority.

66In the past there was a more autocratic type of leadership. The boss was the boss and his authority came with the function. Today the organisation decides whether it will accept the leader or not, and the authority comes from the way people see him or her behaving. These days the leader does less controlling or policing and more encouraging and facilitating. **99**
(Gerard van den Akker, Chairman of The Netherlands Export Combination and winner of the 1991 European Quality Award for Leadership)

HOW TO BE A DISEMPOWERING LEADER

Graham Pitts, training operations manager at W H Smith, devised the UK retailer's New Leadership Change programme. He and his colleagues identified 10 elements of disempowering leadership:

- Stay separate from those you lead
- Avoid being vulnerable by pretending to be confident and knowing the answers
- Don't admit mistakes and so appear defensive
- Expect to be attacked
- Overwork
- Manipulate situations to get things done
- Rely heavily on criticism and rarely praise
- Assume there is a conflict between different groups and so create win–lose situations
- Pursue power rather than purpose

CREATIVE TEAMS

Everyone is creative and all tasks require some degree of creativity. However, some teams are focused mainly on being creative, such as research and development groups, advertising teams, problem-solving taskforces, new product development departments, media programme makers, and so on.

Harnessing the power of creative teams means understanding certain issues critical to the success of such groups. These include allowing freedom, providing creative support, and shielding from outside pressures.

Creative teams are constantly under pressure to produce high-quality results, often extremely quickly. You can help such teams perform by arranging to maximise their freedom, within the constraints of the organisation or the situation. Freedom can mean anything from people choosing their own objectives, to deciding what methods to adopt or hours to work.

You cannot instruct the team to have freedom — people conclude it is theirs for the taking. In essence, you find ways to develop a climate in which people feel they have permission to perform creatively. You actively encourage them through supporting a commitment to constant experimentation, exploring the limits of personal skills, encouraging people to discover what others in their field are doing and meeting different people.

Creative people are constantly kicking against rules and other organisational constraints. You can help them by enabling them to see the constraints as challenges, rather than restrictions. For example, by interpreting limited resources as a challenge to innovate.

"Creative teams run hot and cold. If creative solutions are critical, it may be necessary to run parallel teams. **"**
(Gareth Jones, Senior Vice President,
Human Resources at Polygram International)

It also helps if you can play a number of different leadership roles while harnessing the creative team's power. In all effective teams the leadership moves around to some extent. In creative groups this happens more often and usually faster, as different people produce new thinking or different approaches. Sometimes in these situations effective leadership is simply standing back and not getting in the way.

Some of the traditional team requirements become sharply heightened in a creative group. For example, people play varying roles according to the circumstances, and there is a high degree of trust with people interacting a great deal and depending heavily on each other.

The support you offer any team is important — it is vital to the survival of a creative team. Creative people are often highly self-motivated, yet can rapidly fall into despondency. Despite their creative talents they may be insecure and feel they are only as good as their last job. As their leader, you can support them partly through understanding the roller-coaster nature of the creative cycle and providing the encouragement to bounce back.

SUPPORT

Another aspect of support is providing constant stimulation to think differently and look at the world in new, often surprising ways. Creative teams will often see you as an inspiring leader simply by your offering a constant flow of stimulation and challenge.

It is particularly important too that people learn to build on each other's ideas rather than knock them down. Many new ideas arise almost instantaneously, yet it may take the whole team to construct a workable solution.

So, for example, consider whether some of the present organisational practices help or hinder the development and implementation of ideas. Some companies require reams of paper and supporting material before they will even consider a new product idea. In the 3M company, renowned for its leadership of creative groups, one manager explained that to start a new product development activity, 'Almost one coherent line on a single piece of paper is enough.'

Creativity thrives through many means and often quite simple measures constitute support. For example, giving people plenty of protected physical space, pampering through providing tea or evening meals, using flipcharts, and minimising the bureaucracy.

Imagination is a 200-strong design service based in London whose activities are wide ranging, from corporate communications to exhibitions, product launches, stage lighting and spectaculars.

It is common for 'imagineers', as the employees are called, to work around the clock. The building and the staff restaurant on the ground floor are open 24 hours a day. But the restaurant is more than an amenity. It is a focal point for the networking process that drives Imagination.

'There's a lot of informal mingling in the restaurant,' says Client Services Director Richard Zucker. 'People from different parts of the company get talking about things they've seen or heard, or stuff they're doing that might have a bearing on something else that's going on. That might spark off a new idea, or a new way of doing things on some quite unrelated project.'

Effective team leaders are in any case sensitive to the needs and moods of the individual members. In creative teams this sensitivity is heightened. If you 'see' where people are at, you have a better chance of helping them fully use their creative talents.

RESPONSIBILITY

Successful creative groups often report that their leader gives them considerable amounts of responsibility. Their leaders continually test the team's boundaries and limitations. Along with freedom to succeed and take responsibility, there is also the freedom to make mistakes.

When teams are acting creatively you will often hear people say things like 'I'll take care of that,' 'Let me be responsible for that,' 'Leave that to me.' You can encourage this important process by allowing people to feel they have permission to behave and talk that way.

In many successful creative teams there is no division of roles into people who do the boring bits and those who do the glamorous work. Everyone is expected to do anything that needs doing. Experienced leaders of creative teams argue that the main way to manage them is never to let them get bored with what they are doing. There has to be a constant process of renewal and change.

While all teams are creative, ones that are primarily designed for that purpose have a definite 'yes' culture. There can be considerable tension between a team that keeps saying 'yes' to new ideas and the rest of the organisation which may be more cautious.

CULTURE

To harness the power of the creative team you may have to straddle both strands of the organisation. The traditional part will expect you to do all the right things associated with good management, including not rocking the boat, taking things seriously, being cautious about experiments, and minimising errors.

The creative strand, though, demands that you tap people's creative energies, allow them to make mistakes, challenge traditional ways of doing things and not take life too seriously. Simply by displaying a good sense of humour you are contributing greatly to their effectiveness.

As a champion of your creative team, you need to accept that they are different and may have special needs. So you will have to fight for them to acquire special pay, benefits and facilities that support their creativity. Then you will have to deal with the resentment this causes in those who are not team members.

This sense of being different may pervade the creative team. It may also surface in different dress codes, office arrangements, noticeboards, patterns of work, ways of talking to each other and to the leader, humour, and so on. The team may thus have its own highly individual culture that constantly runs the risk of clashing with the main organisational one.

The sense of difference may mean that the team feels it is not working in an environment receptive to its contribution. So one of the simplest roles you can play is providing an outlet for their frustrations.

PRESSURE

Creative teams are expected to perform. What they have to deliver is often expressed in much tougher terms than is the case for more traditional teams. For example, a media group devising an advertising campaign is expected not only to produce a series of brilliant ideas, but to weld these together into a coherent concept, yet do it to an extremely tight deadline.

The pressure to perform is both stimulating and sometimes deadly. It can provoke supreme effort and, if too sustained, cause burn-out. As ambassador of your creative team, resist excessively tight deadlines or constraints that kill off creative flair.

You will also have to handle the sceptics who question the worth of the group. So, for example, you may need to shield the team from dealing with all sorts of critics, and on its behalf handle the mounds of paperwork that creative people would see as boring or irrelevant.

To handle the pressure from outside your team will want you to be a 'fix-it' person. They will look to you to deal with all sorts of outside distractions and encroachments on the team that could prevent it from focusing on its core task.

Another important action is to ensure the team is having plenty of play and fun. This is when creativity flourishes naturally. If the team is forced to hide its fun and play because this conflicts with what is happening in the rest of the organisation, you may have to take it on regular away days.

ACTION POINTS

 Assume that teams do not always work better than single individuals

 For deciding whether tasks are best done by a team or an individual, use the criteria of uncertainty and the need to share

Select tasks for the team that involve a great deal of uncertainty

 Where the level of uncertainty is low, consider using an individual instead of a team

 Make a task a team effort if it requires people to share knowledge, skills or some other jointly owned resource

 Select tasks for informal groups that use their creative flair, commitment to enjoyment of being together, and their informality in challenging rules

 Consider giving long-term tasks to teams, short-term tasks to individuals

 Consider directing complex tasks to teams and simple tasks to individuals

 In creating sub-teams set clear time limits for their existence and insist these are honoured

 Creative teams require special leadership attention to be given to freedom; the role of the leader; support; responsibility; and shielding the team from outside pressures

13 *How to Survive Multicultural Teams*

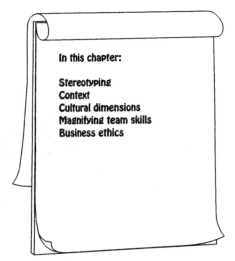

In this chapter:

Stereotyping
Context
Cultural dimensions
Magnifying team skills
Business ethics

The captain of a sinking liner had to get the passengers of various European nationalities to abandon ship into an uninviting sea. Being versed in multicultural matters he divided them up into national groups. To the British he said it was the sporting thing to do, to the French that it was the smart thing to do, to the Germans that it was an order, and to the Italians that it was completely forbidden.

This story reminds us of how we easily we can fall into the trap of using stereotypes to describe people from different nationalities. Many of the stereotypes obstruct our understanding and valuing of the true differences between people.

Fortunately, we do not have to rely entirely on stereotypes to get to grips with some of the more important differences. In recent years many multicultural teams have been established and have thrived. There has also been a growing body of research on improving our understanding of cultural differences.

Our team is a group of individuals with a given expertise under a strong leader with specific objectives and a recognised place in the overall organisation. Our desire to be methodical means we expect to work within the hierarchy. Our leader are strong, decisive and people who know what they are talking about. We naturally defer to their authority and not many people will contradict or criticise them. We obey orders because of the boss's functional role and competence.

Our team is a collection of specialists chosen for their competence in a given field. Our professional relationships are based on rivalry rather than collaboration and we have strong vertical hierarchies. We have an unequivocal leader who in many countries would be regarded as dictatorial. However, our respect for authority is based solidly on our respect for the person's competence.

Our team is really a committee. Even detailed decisions may have to wait for formal approval by the team. There are many other committees we relate to and need to satisfy. We like working to a common goal and there is a large element of self-sacrifice and duty. Individuals are accountable for their actions, so when things go wrong we look for a scapegoat, rather than making sure it does not happen again. Our leader's job is to embody our collective will and take personal responsibility for results.

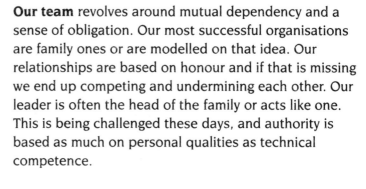

Our team revolves around mutual dependency and a sense of obligation. Our most successful organisations are family ones or are modelled on that idea. Our relationships are based on honour and if that is missing we end up competing and undermining each other. Our leader is often the head of the family or acts like one. This is being challenged these days, and authority is based as much on personal qualities as technical competence.

Our team is a group of powerful individualists in a hierarchy. Power is what matters, measured by how much business you control. We have many titles to distinguish one member from another. Leadership is firmly based on individual accountability. Bosses are like football coaches, giving clear direction rather than consulting, though this is increasingly being challenged. They do not expect us to argue or disagree openly and do not expect consensus. They expect wholehearted commitment to decisions and for us to be fully responsible for our actions.

Our team might seem a bit anarchic, but that is because we see collaboration in terms of voicing an opinion, rather than arriving at decisions and implementing them. Our team is more like a forum to express ideas, of which one will be chosen. Our ideal leader is a benevolent autocrat who has the courage to make sense of all the diverse opinions and then act. The leader has authority not so much from status as from the quality of personal relationships with subordinates.

Culture is 'how we do things around here'. It consists of important assumptions, values and beliefs which decide what happens within a team, an organisation, a geographical area. Culture, therefore, has all sorts of unspoken assumptions that are taken for granted.

An Italian team member, for example, may gladly share feelings and if angry storm out of the meeting without expecting to be unduly criticised for it. This behaviour would not go down well with a German team member.

An American leader will usually consider it useful to hold team sessions that explore mistakes so they can be avoided in the future. In a German team such feedback sessions are seen as an enforced admission of failure. What a British team finds inspiring, a team from another culture may regard as depressing. A Japanese team will spend far longer on obtaining an apparent consensus than most European or American teams.

We grow up in a particular culture and for us our assumptions about how to behave are 'invisible', because we do not see them as anything other than normal. To others they may appear strange, perverse or unacceptable.

Hidden assumptions can undermine your ability to lead through believing that what works for you will also work for other people. An American team leader, for instance, was waxing lyrical about the benefits of networking. This, he argued, was how you got things done in today's modern corporation. To his surprise, an Italian colleague totally disagreed. In Italy, she explained, it was important to work through the hierarchy, not around it as implied by networking.

CONTEXT

Many team leaders increasingly face the challenge of working and surviving in a multicultural context. Swiss managers take charge of French firms, Italian leaders acquire Belgium companies, Swedish executives guide their colleagues in Britain, British project managers steer a group drawn from half a dozen nations. Even within one country a team in Birmingham, for instance, might include Asians, Sikhs and a rich mixture of nationalities including Irish and Welsh people.

It can be a minefield for the uninitiated.

Business is becoming more and more global. In Europe, leadership often means cutting across national cultures. It is harder to think just of a British manager or a French manager. Equally, it is becoming harder to accept uncritically some of the assumptions, even the terminology, drawn mainly from North America.

Words like quality, empowerment or participation can mean entirely different things to each person in a multicultural setting. For example, a Japanese team working with teams from France and Italy may need to check out carefully their mutual assumptions about communication, conflict and control.

Even simple assumptions like how long to take for lunch can prove contentious. The French prefer long lunch breaks, while the English are often satisfied with sandwiches. Emotions play a much larger part in some cultures than others. In an Italian team occasionally shouting at each other and expressing strong views accompanied with much gesticulation is considered normal. It would be frowned on in an Austrian team.

European team leaders who work across national borders must think cross-culturally. They must ask themselves whether a particular approach to organising work, to motivation, to communication, will work with colleagues from other countries with differing cultures.

Many organisations are value driven. There is likely also to be a growing emphasis on establishing policies and procedures that are flexible enough to be translated into different national cultures, yet still be acceptable to local staff.

In summary, therefore, some of our pet theories and ways of managing may not be fully portable from one culture to another. To survive leading a multicultural team you have to look carefully at your assumptions and those of your organisation.

CULTURAL DIMENSIONS

Because the multicultural team has many dimensions, it is important to learn about these before jumping to conclusions. For instance, as a team leader you can quickly become offended, frustrated, or even angry at someone's behaviour when in fact you have simply misunderstood them.

It is not just the words people speak. Body language,

dress, etiquette, hairstyle, ideas, what people think is important, hours of work can all make leading a multicultural team a real challenge.

Because you cannot measure the cultural dimension and its impact, it can be hard for some leaders to get to grips with what may seem a fuzzy sort of issue. It is hard to pin down precisely what to do in what circumstances.

Some of the more obvious dimensions can be seen in an organisational context. For example, you may consider your team as a system for making something happen, a logical mechanism that can be analysed and controlled. Yet this may not work particularly well if some team members see it as more organic, based around relationships.

These different approaches influence how you might tackle a whole range of team tasks including forecasting, decision making, supervision, control, communication, reward and motivation.

While the concept of a team is common to most organisations, structure and purpose differ widely. So, for example, the systematic dimension of a team means that you see people as an assembly of specialists, while in the organic dimension the composition and purpose may be more creative and less clearly defined.

Similarly, the systematic dimension means that people expect meetings to produce tangible results and concrete actions. By contrast, the more organic dimension implies that people will be happy with less tangible outcomes, regarding the meeting as successful if there is mutual understanding and a strengthened will to cooperate.

While there are no rules about surviving in the multicultural team that work regardless of who is in it, there are common areas to focus on:

- Relationships with people
- Relationships to time
- Relations between people and the natural environment

Cultural dimensions

What importance do team members attach to rules rather than maintaining relationships?

Which does the team consider more important, the group or the individual?

To what extent is it OK for this team to express feelings, and which ones?

How far are team members meant to be involved with important decisions?

In a genuinely multicultural team one might assume that many of the differences will simply cancel each other out. Given the impossibility of anticipating and understanding every cultural nuance, it might even seem sensible simply to lead without any regard to cultural dimensions.

This approach is likely to hit difficulties sooner, rather than later. A better solution is to stay intensely attuned to what your team needs to work well together. This means being more than usually alert to what is happening within the team, assessing the work processes and adjusting your responses accordingly.

Advice points

> You cannot assume that people have the same views about 'what is a team', so put this on the agenda right away.
>
> Since people probably have divergent views, experiences and assumptions, explore these early in the life of your team.
>
> ● Ask team members to define what they mean by a team
> ● Explain how you as a leader expect to see this team function
> ● Offer ground rules such as:
> – specific ways of working
> – how instructions or orders will be communicated
> – ways in which people are expected to communicate

The alertness you need to apply in such teams may be at the expense of spending more time on your own specialist expertise. In single nationality teams, the leader also often plays an additional expert role contributing towards delivering an important team result. For example, you may be an expert in forecasting. However, in a multicultural team, be prepared to devote a much greater proportion of your time to staying alert and helping to foster teamwork.

MAGNIFIED TEAM SKILLS

Even if you are well read and widely travelled, it is unlikely that you can fully understand the cultural context and traditions of everyone in a fully multicultural team. One clear principle to emerge from people's practical experience of leading such teams is the necessity to magnify your team skills.

In a multicultural team you will need to be much more focused on ways of applying team leadership skills and adopting appropriate techniques. For example, in a monocultural team the pace and time of work may be generally taken for granted by everyone. In a multicultural team, you will have to slow down to perhaps 75 per cent of the pace you might expect in a team of one culture. Allowing enough time should be built into the rules of engagement that the team defines at the outset.

So, for instance, allow plenty of time for people to learn to communicate with each other, and to sort out misunderstandings and resolve conflicts. You may have to be much more available to help individuals cope with the cross-cultural context and handle the difficulties it causes them.

This does not necessarily mean that the team runs at a snail's pace. It does imply that you must be patient about how fast you can expect the team to go. For example, in some multicultural teams you will have to allow time for translations to occur. You may also need to allow the team to work through issues more thoroughly to avoid misunderstanding.

CONTRACT BUILDING

It is important to establish clear contracts between people, not in the legal sense, but in how they will work together. For example, it will help if you gain agreement on all the key values that will guide the team's work and its relationships.

You cannot assume that the key values have the same meaning for everyone and may have to spend time ensuring there is a common understanding. Terms like honesty, openness, working to deadlines can be interpreted entirely differently depending on one's culture.

If the multicultural team is expected to work together for a year or more, it will certainly pay to have quarterly team development sessions. Rather than focusing on the day-to-day work, these concentrate on team building, developing relationships and enhancing team practice.

In between, create weekly team meetings of around half an hour to sort out the smaller issues that constantly crop up in such teams. A useful approach is to have these sessions led each week by a representatives from different cultures. This way people get to see how others think and operate.

Particularly in multicultural teams it really pays to focus your team leadership efforts on helping people have fun together. As one experienced British project manager leading a multicultural team in Munich puts it, 'Fun must be managed.'

Create social events for the team, so people really get to know each other and the barriers can begin to come down. These events will not necessarily happen regularly, unless you or a team member takes responsibility for seeing that they do. People are often extremely proud of their culture and enjoy sharing this with others. For example, if the multicultural team is based in Germany let the Germans entertain the rest of the team with a typical German night out.

Unless they come from Denmark, Luxembourg or the Netherlands, most people are unlikely to be able to follow a simple conversation in a language other than their own. The European Union has nine official languages and a large number of dialects. Ideally, as a leader of a multicultural team you need to acquire at least a smattering of languages that would be relevant to your team. This may not matter much if you are only dealing with senior managers, but if you have acquired a factory or are setting up a local team it may be a significant problem.

LONGER-TERM ACTION

MAKE IT FUN

THE VIRTUAL TEAM

A growing number of companies are creating 'virtual teams' drawn from different countries and different organisations. Strategic alliances and joint ventures force-feed the creation of multicultural teams that must work well together through electronic media, while people hardly ever meet face to face.

The virtual team can be a network of suppliers, customers, even erstwhile rivals, linked by information technology to share skills, costs and access to one another's markets. Leading such disparate teams and producing worthwhile results may demand the development of a whole new range of management skills.

AT&T used Japan's Marubeni Trading company to link up with Matsushita Electrical Industrial company in order to jump start the production of its Safari notebook computer, designed by yet another company.

MCI Communications uses as many as 100 companies to win major contracts with large customers. IBM, Apple and Motorola are all experimenting with virtual teams that cross local, national and international boundaries.

Learning the basics of all the languages present in the team is a good way of maintaining the bond within it. It can also be great fun as a game in the starting stage of the team's development. Encourage members to do this and correct them in a supportive way. This actively demonstrates a caring relationship that distinguishes team members from others.

While the international context is important, it may not be the biggest cause of difficulty. There is an increasing gap between those who have received professional training and those who have not. For instance, many professional managers under 40 have been exposed to American business methods and outlook. Their approach can weld a multicultural team together rapidly and just as easily cause problems for certain older members who are less familiar with such methods.

The attitudes to women held by both sexes seem to

come mainly from their perceived role outside the workplace, rather than inside it. So if you are leading a multicultural team with women members, you can be fairly sure that issues of particular importance to women apply across the cultural divide: combining family and career, maternity leave, provision of childcare facilities, the need to do as well as equivalent men, and so on.

BUSINESS ETHICS

You may face issues about honesty, integrity and what is 'right and wrong'. This is another minefield since social values differ widely across cultures, and attitudes to government, family, local community, employer and employee are diverse.

Some members of your team might, for example, believe that lavish expenses and tax-deductible entertainment are perfectly normal, indeed expected. Some members of the team may expect to award an important contract to a close family member or friend, while other members would be shocked at such behaviour.

Your job is to help the team establish its ground rules so that the working relationships are viable and based on trust. The Starting and Sorting Stages of team development discussed in Chapter 6 may therefore take on added significance in the multicultural team.

While being aware of the cultural and ethical differences is the first step in being able to handle them, there is a second more important one. This is your active demonstration of this awareness. The subsequent empathy this engenders will help build and maintain trust.

One of the results of allowing time for the team to get acquainted is that you can decide how best to deal with the inevitable concerns that people may have about working together in a multicultural context. For instance, while it may be helpful to encourage people to have a formal session to share these anxieties, such openness in public may be alien to some team members. The best place to air these worries may turn out to be over a good meal.

As leader of a multicultural team you will be faced with diversity and need to learn to respect it. Valuing the differences between people is a basic survival requirement for leading such a team. Since there is no one 'right way' to lead, part of the secret of first survival and then success is recognising the cultural dimension.

However, one of the strange findings from multicultural research is that the more you know, the harder it may make be to lead a multicultural team well. This probably reflects the fact that a little knowledge can be a dangerous thing. Being aware of cultural differences does not necessarily mean you automatically know how to handle them well.

Take relationships, for example. It is fine to realise that a Japanese team expects to spend hours or days consulting everyone. This might lead you to avoid going for quick results. Yet while this might be right nine times out of ten, actual experience suggests that sometimes such teams welcome someone coming from outside who can help them get more directly to the final decision.

Leading multicultural teams can therefore be complex. It really pays to begin clarifying *how* you intend to lead the team. For example, you may come from a culture that likes to structure meetings with clear time boundaries, set agreed intervals for breaks and issue definite agendas. Others in your team may come from countries where meetings usually flow with only an occasional nudge to give them direction. They can often come to accept your new ground rules, once they have understood that this is the new context in which they are expected to work.

TIPS FROM THE SURVIVORS

Advice points

- *Visual aids* — Use lots of visual aids in the multicultural team. Adopt cartoons and pictures to communicate important points: people tend to relate to them.
- *Signals* — Try giving every team member a red and a yellow card. When they hold up the red one it means 'I don't understand.' When they hold up the yellow one it means 'You're ignoring me.
- *Grudge bag session* — Experiment with the grudge bag idea. You regularly invite people to 'unload their sack of grudges' onto the team table and discuss what is niggling them. You might even put up a picture of a rucksack to symbolise the session. This way you will catch many misunderstandings that would otherwise fester and damage team performance.
- *Open agenda meetings* — Hold weekly open sessions in which there is no specific topic on the agenda. Allow people to speak about only non-technical matters and prevent any one person from dominating. Use the open agenda to determine whether or not mutual understanding has been attained. The team may continue to move towards the desired goal yet not entirely reach it because the misunderstanding was identified too late.
- *Glossary of terms* — For longer-term teams, create a glossary of terms that can be used across cultural boundaries. Terms like 'product group' and 'reasons for issuing a credit note' may need to be carefully defined to establish a common terminology. In Sweden an invoice is something you pay, in Italy it is something you negotiate.

ACTION POINTS

 Check out mutual assumptions in the multicultural team

 Be prepared for the team to move more slowly than a monocultural team

 Encourage people to become better acquainted through socialising and relaxation periods

 Be willing to start learning at least some of the languages used in your team

 Help the team create its own ground rules so that working relationships are viable and based on trust

 Establish ways of identifying when the team's ground rules have been broken, and when this happens endorse ownership and acceptability of the rules

 Valuing the differences and actively demonstrating your appreciation is a basic survival tactic

 Being aware of cultural differences is not the same as knowing how handle them

 Early in the life of the team clarify for people how you intend to lead it

 In looking for cultural implications consider:
- relationships between people and the team as a whole
- relationships to time
- relations between people and the natural environment

Stay constantly alert to what is happening in the team; avoid getting too involved with your own specialist function

 Ask team members to define what they mean by a team

 Explain how you as a leader expect to see this team function

 Offer ground rules such as:
- specific ways of working
- how instructions or orders will be communicated
- ways in which people are expected to communicate

14 *Team Characteristics*

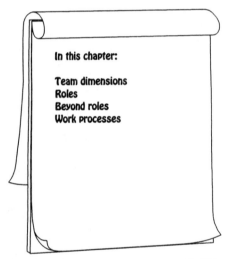

In this chapter:

Team dimensions
Roles
Beyond roles
Work processes

Like individuals, teams have their own personalities. This is often what distinguishes teams from each other. A team can mean different things to different people. Trainers, developers, leaders, policy makers, consultants and team members may vary considerably in how they see a particular team. Cultural differences add another layer.

For example, what does 'leader' or 'mutual support' really mean? It varies across different companies and cultures. Can we even define 'team' satisfactorily? Beyond language and its endless scope for misunderstanding, if you lead a team or help others develop theirs it is useful to have a framework for thinking about them in a coherent, rounded way.

DIMENSIONS

Team leaders used to have only two dimensions to their job: managing the task and managing the people. Many felt comfortable with the former, and rather less so with the latter. More recently, a third dimension has emerged. This is the role of client or business manager, and focuses on delivering high value to customers. Some organisations are finding the switch a hard one to make. For example, if you order a new business phone system from British Telecom, you deal with one part of the company. Yet they pass you to a different branch to have a fax line installed. To the average customer this approach is more for BT's benefit than theirs.

After virtually losing control of its purpose and direction during the 1980s, IBM became committed in the early 1990s to running different parts of its company as businesses in their own right. Each one is accountable for its own success and profitability. Given this extra dimension of the leadership job, the tasks of planning, organising, coordination, controlling and motivating become harder, even impossible. There are simply insufficient hours in the day for one person to do them unaided.

Faced with these challenges, many organisations are gradually handing back authority and responsibility to employees and hence teams. There is nothing idealistic about this trend. It is a survival tactic for the fewer, remaining managers and leaders.

This new degree of complexity also means many leaders have concluded that they need to understand more about their team and the individual characteristics of their team members.

ROLES

The focus on team characteristics stems from studies in the late 1940s. These looked at the dynamics of small groups and identified some easy-to-understand roles. For example, people in groups were classified as Playboy, Dominator, Recognition Seeker, Aggressor and so on.

Games

In the 1970s, Meredith Belbin used business games to develop a way of describing team roles. He concluded that successful teams need a balanced mixture of roles. Most team developers are now at least familiar with his nine team roles.

Belbin's classification system is still used for helping teams think about roles and their effectiveness. For example, IBM taught the Belbin approach for 10 years on its personal skills development courses. Other systems, such as the Margerison and McCann Team Index, also use psychological profiling to classify people.

Unfortunately labelling people is not particularly helpful for leading a team, although it does provide a common language for talking about how people behave. Roles are simple to understand, however, since they focus on an individual.

The simplicity of individual roles is attractive and many developers and leaders use the idea as a way of persuading teams to take a closer look at how they are working together.

Classifying team members by role is so easy it tends to obscure two basic issues: does it really work, and is it useful?

An unpublished 1993 IBM study about the company's use of Belbin's system reported that it was hardly used outside the classroom. The researcher asked pointedly: 'If we are teaching it, then why are we not using it?' Those who watched the steady decline of IBM in the 1980s could be forgiven for wondering whether the 10 years of teaching managers in the classroom about roles did IBM any good at all.

If you use the role method for exploring your team's characteristics you will quickly discover its limitations. You have little scope for using the results for continuous team improvement and it seldom makes sense to repeat it. As the Head of Human Resources for Harlow Council puts it, 'After you've assessed roles there is a large element of: so what?'

TEAM ROLES

Belbin roles
- Plant
- Resource Investigator
- Co-ordinator
- Shaper
- Monitor Evaluator
- Team Worker
- Implementer
- Completer-Finisher
- Specialist

Margerison and McCann
- Creator Innovator
- Explorer Promoter
- Assessor Developer
- Thruster Organiser
- Concluder Producer
- Controller Inspector
- Upholder Maintainer
- Reporter Advisor
- Linker

Roles are only partially helpful in analysing a team because of what happens in the real world. A team often faces a major challenge, such as working to a demanding deadline, achieving outstanding sales, resolving a significant problem, dealing with a threat to its survival or main purpose. In such situations teams usually abandon fixed roles. Previously firm barriers separating individual roles often disappear. As one experienced executive sees it, 'When the shit hits the fan, Belbin goes out the window.'

Another reason why the use of roles is so limited is the underlying assumption that teams should have a careful mix of roles. Yet few people have the luxury of appointing their team entirely from scratch. Even when you can do so, it usually proves difficult or impossible to create a neat balance of roles.

A more fundamental weakness of role analysis is its narrow focus on the individual, rather than the team. You need a way of looking at the team as a whole, rather than as separate members. Roles are more like labels than useful explanations of how to achieve results.

BEYOND ROLES

An alternate approach is to focus on specific team problems. By taking known team issues such as 'team members do not get on with the leader', you can create a range of possible team actions. Although you need a large list of such problems to make this approach work, it does at least tap into a team's real experience. Because the members recognise the issues, they may be more willing to explore what to do about them.

However, the issue-based method is still a fragmented one. It does not look at the team as a whole. You do not emerge with a particularly meaningful picture of your team. Nor does it help you compare how the team is changing over time.

WORK METHODS (PROCESSES)

Seminal studies in the early 1960s suggested that groups experience various phases of maturity, similar to those of a human being. Teams that go through these phases are usually more successful than those that do not. Our own approach, outlined in Chapter 6, uses the six phases of Starting, Sorting, Stabilising, Striving, Succeeding and Stopping. These are not always entirely distinct, often merging imperceptibly from one to another.

If a team has a natural life cycle, a more rounded way of analysing what is happening at any one moment is to focus on *how* the people work together. This focuses on 'what happens when we are working together'.

Team leaders, developers and consultants are increasingly adopting study of work methods for exploring the characteristics of teams. It help them understand what is happening 'in the moment', to realise how people are interacting. This is probably the closest you can get to observing the whole team in action.

Indeed, team members often talk about themselves by describing processes, saying things like: 'We really support each other in our team,' 'Our team is highly creative,' 'We're really hot on having clear objectives,' 'There is no doubt about who's leading our team.'

By exploring how the team works together, the focus stays on what people are doing jointly. It is a fuller, more satisfying way to judge both current effectiveness and the need for any future changes.

Our own approach draws on both the ideas above and the experience of successful teams in the theatre and the performing arts. These teams must often form quickly and produce a high-quality result in weeks, rather than months. We describe a successful, powerful team as Aligned, Creative and Exploring. These are explained further in Chapter 7.

TO SUM UP

There are endless classifications, models and descriptions of teams. Those at the sharp end of a team — trainers, policy makers and team members — may conclude that these are too remote from their own reality. Certainly there are so many variables affecting an individual team's performance that no single approach is likely to provide a definitive answer to creating a winning team. In some situations a role analysis may help, in others it may merely be a waste of time.

Trainers wanting to enhance team working need to test out different approaches, evaluating them carefully, rather than taking on trust some of the more popular ones. Policy makers may find little to attract them in arcane discussions about the usefulness or otherwise of roles and work methods. Instead, they need to keep their focus on team performance, on outcomes and effectiveness. Astute leaders should keep exploring different approaches to see what works well for them and their particular team. Above all, they must keep looking, learning as we suggest in an earlier chapter to *see* what is happening and what is needed.

15 *A Strategic View of Teams*

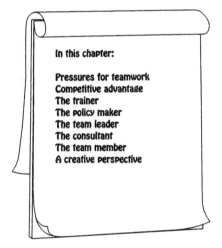

In this chapter:

Pressures for teamwork
Competitive advantage
The trainer
The policy maker
The team leader
The consultant
The team member
A creative perspective

Planning to drive from, say, Birmingham to Istanbul involves a great deal of preparation. You will need several maps, including one of Europe giving an overview of the whole journey, and several others showing the detailed roads within each country. The destination may be clear, but how to get there requires a plan.

Strategy is a jargon word for the route map of how to gain advantage over your competitors. A team strategy is therefore concerned with the whole picture of how teams and their leaders will contribute to organisational success.

Teams are now firmly on most companies' agendas. Some are realising that they offer an important way of ensuring consistent quality and exceptional results.

Others are further down the road, exploring the wilder side of team working.

Wherever you look, teams seem to be a topic of interest to organisations. This is partly due to their inevitability. If organisations become larger and more complex, teams are the only assured way of combining disparate skills into a powerful force for obtaining exceptional results.

Similarly, when organisations reduce size by eliminating layers of hierarchy, then more responsibility and authority devolve onto those who make things or deliver services. For these organisations too, team working is an important resource they cannot ignore.

In smaller companies, teams frequently define their whole style and approach. People are attracted by the prospect of close working relationships, being creative together, using mutual energy to achieve more than they could do on their own.

The question, therefore, is not so much 'why' team working, as 'how?' Consequently there is continuing and growing interest in what is the best way to lead teams of all kinds.

Competitive advantage is what allows an organisation to thrive — and today it is being eroded in record time. Advantages that last year seemed long-term winners are this year already under attack. The competition gets better and more innovative. For many enterprises the only real competitive advantage left is the special skill and talents of its workforce. In such a world, another critical factor is time. The time available to think of a product or service and get it to market seems constantly to shrink. Only 10 years ago the life cycle for a new computer model was mainly counted in years. Today it is counted in months. A new car used to take the best part of a decade to launch, today it is often only a matter of one or two years.

If people are indeed the organisation's most enduring competitive advantage, then how they are organised to maximise individual and collective potential is also critical. People and their grouping into teams are now increasingly seen as strategic resources. How best to use this strategic resource is a concern not just of team leaders, but others such as trainers, policy makers, consultants and team members.

THE TRAINER

Trainers or personnel experts are expected to offer an understanding of practical ways to develop effective teams. This includes suggesting means to identify and develop competent team leaders. Those with a background in behavioural change will want new ways to promote effective teams, in the light of changing organisational conditions.

Those with a less theoretical training will want to understand what works and what does not, how best to help practising team leaders do their job well, when the job itself may be radically altering in response to market pressures. For example, as we saw in Chapter 5, many manufacturing organisations are exploring the ramifications of self-managing teams. They are seldom doing this solely from sheer intellectual interest. More likely they have learned of the large gains other producers have made from adopting new forms of teams and leadership.

In devising training programmes for enhancing team leadership, it can be tempting to rely on apparently well-tried ideas, such as outward bound courses that claim to develop teams and team leaders rapidly. Increasingly such methods are recognised as oversimplistic.

66Swimming in freezing water at six o'clock every morning did not necessarily make me a better person, just a colder person. **99**
(Manager on an outdoor learning course)

An important attraction of the outdoor style of training is simply its apparent speed. By providing a huge challenge to the participants, some trainers and their clients assume that the resulting camaraderie and personal growth permanently enhance teams and their leadership within the workplace. These assumptions are now being questioned, although the approach has produced some useful results.

> An Industrial Society study in 1994 found that the use of outdoor training for developing teams was losing its previous popularity. It found that while outdoor training does have its place, 'the more macho stuff which is inappropriate for many people is in decline.'

Talking point

To carry weight in the area of developing competent team leaders, trainers require a strategic view of teams. They have to stand back from the attraction of any one supposedly effective development method in favour of gaining a better understanding of what is involved when people work together towards a common goal.

A strategic view also recognises the time it takes for changes to occur. This encourages thought about timing and what are the relevant support structures. Another issue on which trainers may need to give guidance is how best to phase the changes towards team working and improved leadership, for maximum impact.

For trainers to take a strategic view also means taking responsibility for ensuring there exists a permanent link between any training and development and the organisation's business plan. This is difficult enough to do even if you have access to senior management. Yet many trainers are well removed from the rarefied atmosphere of corporate strategy.

To make the links between business strategy and training means first establishing clarity about the business results required, and then analysing how training and development can help achieve them.

LINKS TO BUSINESS PLANS

One of the most systematic examples of a strategic approach was in Woolworths, part of the Kingfisher group. There the policy maker clearly recognised that to revive a moribund, poorly led retail enterprise required a far-reaching investment in training and development, including better leadership. This investment was not seen as an optional extra. The policy maker's plans simply could not be realised without it and the person responsible for the development programme was regarded as central, not marginal, to desired business results.

For trainers to take a strategic view, they must therefore be willing to tackle executive barriers, urging policy makers to communicate what they are trying to achieve. This is soon valued by most policy makers and permits a more detailed exploration of how training and development might contribute.

When in doubt, trainers need to express their uncertainty, even when it challenges apparently well-embedded programmes which have been functioning for a considerable time.

The strategic role takes the trainer beyond the narrow confines of course provider into becoming an organisational change consultant. This is both daunting and exhilarating. Helping the organisation create effective team leaders is one of the most important tasks one can embark on. It may not appeal to everyone.

Without the tight linkage to business strategy, especially in the encouragement of leaders, training and development can soon be marginalised. Regardless of how many courses and development events occur, policy makers quickly realise that these are not contributing to fundamental organisational priorities.

When this occurs, there are only two ways to go. The first is for training and development professionals to stay buried within the organisation, contributing in relatively minor ways. The second is outsourcing, in which frustrated policy makers abandon the struggle to make internal training and development relevant, in favour of outsiders who are prepared to take responsibility for ensuring the tight linkage with corporate strategy.

So trainers and developers must act strategically. Teams and team leadership provide an excellent platform for doing this and being seen to do so. Team leadership can be a spearhead for a trainer or developer to pursue legitimately a whole gamut of organisational change issues. It allows them to review the effectiveness of meetings in the organisation, how people communicate with each other, the quality of joint work with allies and competitors in making commercial bids, and so on.

Thinking and behaving strategically also requires an interest in the structures which will support the training and development effort. This tends to be a neglected area of trainer concern. Too little attention is usually paid, for instance, to identifying what it will take to sustain an investment in developing leaders and their teams over the longer term.

For example, company training programmes often try to develop teams and leaders with only limited commitment from senior managers. The latter have often made all the right noises, and even encouraged the creation of a training programme. Yet they avoid responsibility for vital reinforcing actions such as modelling desired behaviour, providing encouragement, giving feedback, altering methods of remuneration, and so on.

MODELLING

Ray Marlow, founder in 1973 and now chief executive of the Dallas-based semiconductor manufacturer Marlow Industries, warned his 150 staff at one of his monthly meetings that he would occasionally pick on someone to stand up and recite the company's seven quality principles. At a later meeting a young lady took the microphone from him and challenged him to do the same. The deliberately high-profile boss passed the test.

This is a difficult area for in-house professionals to tackle. They may have the uncomfortable task of confronting one or more reluctant, busy senior manager and enrolling them in the change process. Again, doing this can help make the trainer an important organisational change agent — indeed it requires leadership skills in its own right.

We are struck by how many teams of HR specialists in large organisations are themselves poorly led. You cannot be a credible ambassador of teamwork, for example, if your own team is lacking in leadership and disorganised. There is plenty of scope, therefore, for heads of training and personnel to improve their own leadership skills in running their teams.

At the other end of the strategic spectrum, trainers and developers require a bulging toolkit of ideas, methods and systems for helping to make team leadership effective. Many of these are described in this book. While it is unnecessary for trainers and developers to master all of them, it is important that they are aware of what seems to work. One of their most useful contributions to policy makers and line managers who must lead teams is pointing to resources that can make a difference. For example, they can help leaders adopt viable ways of assessing their team and determining the priorities for development.

66As a leader, act as you say; continue to learn, grow, change and encourage others to do the same. **99** (SmithKline Beecham's Group Chairman, Robert Bauman)

THE POLICY MAKER

Strategic thinking for senior managers in the area of teams and team leadership needs to focus on issues such as: whether to adopt team working as a way of running an effective organisation, how better team leadership would contribute to important business goals, how to sustain team working across the organisation, and making sure formal support structures are in place.

Adopting team working either across the whole organisation or in a major part of it, such as on the production floor of a factory, can have major cultural implications. For example, it may mean an entirely new approach to supervision and a new way of integrating previously separate functions.

> In one major British paper-making plant, the decision to introduce self-managing teams not only swept away old supervisory practices, it also required office-based staff to become part of the factory production team. Apart from any natural resistance such new ways or working might bring, it also demanded that senior management rethink their whole approach to supporting and encouraging this change.

It is relatively easy for a policy maker to embrace team working, setting the wheels in motion for it to occur. However, a strategic approach demands more considered action to identify how the leadership will personally relate to the change. For example, how can you modify your own attitude to tolerance of team failure, or avoid criticising that previously came all too naturally?

Another cultural and consequently strategic shift policy makers may need to pursue is in how they view team leaders. For example, the issue of managerial control versus facilitating leadership opens up areas such as the extent and appropriateness of delegation, or the ability of leaders to move from a criticising to an encouraging approach.

It also means policy makers clarifying and sharing their vision of how they see teams and their leaders functioning. For example, in our own company we have tried to describe the way we want the office support team to work, with a commitment to creativity and trying to make their often rather tedious work more tolerable.

As we have seen, there are many types of teams and a wide variety of leadership styles. Policy makers need to enrol people in their view of how things *should* be.

REMUNERATION

In seeking better team leadership, policy makers may also have to give considerable attention to how people are recognised and rewarded. This is not only about appreciating people, it also concerns the prosaic issue of pay. In an organisation that is really concerned with developing effective teamwork, efforts will have to be made to resolve conflicts over individual versus team remuneration.

Many organisations pay lip-service to teamwork while permitting damaging interpersonal competition between individuals, exacerbated by pay differentials. One of the core distinctions of effective teamwork is inter-dependence. It may therefore be necessary to develop new avenues for channelling competitive instincts so that they support rather than detract from sound teamwork.

Remuneration is a strategic issue for which policy makers must take responsibility. This does not concern the details of who receives what, but the underlying principles of how the system will underpin team working and enhance the leader's role. Finally, there is the strategic issue of inter-team working. How do you get different teams, often from different cultures, to work well together? How best can you help those responsible combine diversity into team strength? We cover these issues in Chapter 13.

It is less important for policy makers to offer specific answers to these questions than to be asking them. By showing an awareness of such issues, policy makers help guide and grow the organisation in new ways of thinking and ultimately of working together.

THE TEAM LEADER

Team leaders also benefit from a strategic approach. If they are policy makers in their own right, they face a doubly difficult task. It goes beyond just managing day-to-day business. Strategy for team leaders is concerned with the team's wider role in the organisation and how it is contributing to important goals.

An effective team leader reaches beyond the confines of operational activity to offer a vision of how the group can best work and play together to achieve results. It therefore means taking responsibility for issues such as how to help the team develop a more creative approach, revitalise itself, regularly assess its overall effectiveness, and identify and set team goals.

As a team leader you may have only limited power to alter individual remuneration. Yet this too is an area for concern. It can mean, for example, exploring the limits to how the team as a whole is rewarded and recognised. Committed team leaders will often try to adapt present organisational remuneration systems to suit their particular concern of developing less interpersonal rivalry and more interdependence.

How the team relates to others in the organisation and beyond is yet another aspect of a strategic focus. Active team leaders seldom accept current ways of working as sacrosanct. They want to explore new approaches to inter-team relationships. This often takes them into the difficult territory of cultural change, with all its implications for obtaining support from senior management.

In trying to think strategically, team leaders need to focus on managing change, dealing with uncertainty and handling risk. In such an environment it makes sense to consider such personal issues as 'Who gives me support?', 'What training and development do I need?' and 'How do I relate to other team leaders?'

THE CONSULTANT

Outsiders have traditionally played a considerable role in helping organisations tackle the introduction of teams and the development of their leaders. The contribution has usually been in the form of specialist consultancy, or through providing training and development events. The advantage of outsiders is that they can often see the wood from the trees. This benefit is quickly lost if they become too enmeshed in the organisation and its current concerns.

A strategic approach for consultants means acting partly like a policy maker, asking important questions, and drawing attention to critical issues such as: the need for an effective team-working system, the cultural implications for the organisation of changes in team working, and how best to assess the effectiveness of each team.

Another important contribution is to help trainers, policy makers and team leaders acquire practical ways of enhancing team development and to understand the leadership implications. This means using a coherent and credible set of values about team working and leadership, offering practical ways to translate these into meaningful action. The more academic consultants will also offer an understandable model of team working that incorporates these values and is at least based on some rationale that clients can grasp.

THE TEAM MEMBER

The challenge for the individual is how to be an effective member not only within a single team, but increasingly across several other teams too. In that sense each person needs a personal survival strategy. For example, how do you handle competing loyalties, pressure on your time, different styles of leadership, and so on?

Some of the answers to being an effective team member across several teams are emerging in the skill of networking and learning systematically to build relationships with people from different areas of responsibility or even cultures.

It is naturally difficult for any single team member, apart from its formal leader, to view the team strategically. The best teams consist of members who can look beyond their own immediate role to the overall team role and direction.

Since teams also react with other teams, either internal to the organisation or outside it, individual members may also begin to be concerned with obtaining a more macro picture of effective team working. If your own team can only succeed by working well with others, then it will also matter who is creating obstacles to being effective.

'How can we have better team members?', 'How can we encourage trust?', 'What does the leader require from us?', 'How can I too play a leadership role?' are questions the individual team member can ask and thus show a strategic concern. Asking for opportunities to explore such issues is therefore an important contribution which each person can make to broadening the team's perspective.

The point of truly effective teamwork, especially in self-managing teams, is the empowerment of the individual. In such teams, everyone is concerned to some degree with strategic team issues. So 'our relationships with other teams', 'the way we run meetings in this organisation', 'whether the remuneration system encourages or deters interdependence' cease being matters solely for team leaders or policy makers. Instead they start to concern everyone.

A CREATIVE PERSPECTIVE

One of the great attractions of teams is their ability to be more than the sum of the parts. Well-run teams tend to be more productive and creative than any single member. This synergy not only justifies the existence of teams, it is a major reason for continuing to develop them.

Effective teams can challenge the whole way an organisation achieves results. Once you unleash their true power it is hard to predict exactly where this will take the organisation. This uncertainty can prove uncomfortable for those who insist on knowing the how, when, who and what of any team development programme. Yet the very nature of effective team leadership is to unlock the team's creative strength, and in so doing produce all sorts of unexpected implications.

A well-run team will test to the limits what the organisation will tolerate in terms of change and new ideas. It will challenge the existing rules and question whether the old ways are the best. For example, a proactive team leader will insist on the team exploring all its boundaries, not only within the parent organisation but with outside ones too, such as suppliers and customers. Nominally most policy makers and other senior people welcome this creativity. In practice, it may begin to challenge vested interests.

Managing the creativity released by successful teamwork is a major issue. Once you seriously embark on encouraging it, there is a Pandora's box effect. Having begun the process, it is hard to reverse and the ramifications can seem both endless and formidable.

66You can't control a large organisation like Digital — you can only steer it and try and harness the energy within it, hopefully pointing it in the right direction. **99**
(Senior Digital manager)

For this reason alone, taking a strategic overview of teams is always sensible. You may not know exactly where it will lead, but you can at least become familiar with the territory it is likely to involve.

20 Team Tips that Work 16

1 Leadership. Seek clarity about who is leading the team — sometimes informal leadership moves around the team. Leaders take responsibility for what the team is trying to achieve.

2 Inspiration. If you want to inspire your team, first inspire yourself. When you successfully communicate your own passion for something you care about, it fires up other people too.

3 Task and process. High performance teams focus intently on their task, yet also find time to keep reviewing their performance by examining the processes they are using.

4 Listening. Encourage listening by asking anyone wanting to speak to:

- Sum up what the previous person just said
- Say how their comments link to the previous contribution

5 Deadlines. Push for clear deadlines which are rarely abandoned or changed.

6 Goals. Teams thrive on clear goals. Use SMART goals which are:

- Stretching
- Measurable
- Agreed
- Recorded
- Time limited

7 Challenge. People respond to challenges which stretch their abilities and tap into their natural creativity. Ensure that challenges for your team are demanding.

8 Feelings. Regularly (e.g. once a week) start a meeting by inviting people to share how they are feeling, including anything which could stop them being effective in the meeting.

9 Relationships. Promote team relationships and the development of mutual trust by:

- encouraging frank, no-holds-barred discussions
- not avoiding conflict
- acknowledging strong feelings
- working on tasks jointly

10 Meetings. Regularly (at one- to four-weekly intervals) bring the whole team together. It cannot be a team if people are isolated and only make contact by phone, memo or quick chats in the corridor.

11 Agendas. Team meetings need proper agendas. Create ones which clearly state:

- Topic — the issue
- Initiator — person wanting it tabled
- Purpose — what it is broadly about
- Timescale — amount of time it will require
- Outcome — for decision, discussion or information

12 Chairing. Always have team meetings with a facilitator or chairperson, responsible for:

- encouraging both task and process
- seeing there is a proper agenda or logical flow
- allowing enough time for each issue
- ensuring everyone gains a hearing
- keeping the meeting to time

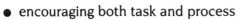

13 Tasks. Each team member needs to understand how they can contribute to success. Make tasks well defined, so people can play their full part.

14 Celebrate. Search for frequent opportunities to celebrate success in your team. Use the occasion to give everyone public recognition.

15 Chunk it. When the team faces a major task, break it into more manageable stages, each with its own start and finishing time.

16 Transition. Help the team understand what stage of development it has reached. Try asking members to share their view of what stage the team has reached.

17 Minutes. Good teams keep action minutes which show everyone:

- What was decided
- Who will do what
- By when

18 Delegate. Make sure everyone in the team has a role which fully stretches them as a human being. Check with each person regularly whether they can take more responsibility and if so, give it to them.

19 Blockages. A team leader should regularly ask the team:

- What specifically can I do to make your job easier, more enjoyable, more satisfying?

Team members should regularly ask the leader:

- What specifically can we do to help you be a more effective team leader, and do your job better?

20 Vision. Check that everyone in the team holds the same picture of what team success would look and feel like if it was achieved.

Virtual Teams 17

Nobody said running a team had to be easy, but virtual teams are truly tough. Nevertheless they do offer definite benefits while creating their own kind of leadership challenges and their number is increasingly rapidly.

While such teams seem new there have always been careers where individuals operated far from colleagues and managers. Missionaries, for example, came home every seven years. In the diplomatic service, Beijing embassy staff may never even meet their regular contacts in Washington or London.

Globalisation, mergers and acquisitions force-fed the emergence of new kinds of dispersed teams, where people worked in remote locations yet had to stay in close touch. These remote teams were hard to manage simply because there were so few tools to help bind the groups together, apart from shared objectives and maybe a corporate culture.

Then advances in communications technology made remote, virtual teams far more viable. And it is the technology that often dominates, vacuuming up large amounts of leadership time and energy. Yet doing this loses sight of the fundamental requirement to focus on the human aspects of the virtual group. No matter how brilliant the technology, your role as a leader is to concentrate on getting the best from your team. You can't do that if you are beguiled by the technology, becoming absorbed in its ramifications.

Many non-technology factors drive the continuing growth of virtual teams. These include the rising cost of office space, flexible work patterns, service providers aligning to customers by working inside their organisations, pressure on labour costs through contract workers and part-timers and so on.

Even relatively small companies find they like the results of using virtual teams. Leading these teams demands new skills, however, particularly having a highly responsive and flexible style in managing the membership.

WHAT MAKES A VIRTUAL TEAM?

- Dispersal: people work in multiple locations.
- Empowerment: shared powers, responsibilities and accountabilities.
- Restlessness: people accept and seem enthusiastic for change.
- Interdependence: cooperation and synergy between people and across organisations.
- Technology: plays a major role in binding people together.
- Shared purpose: which everyone understands and buys into.
- Trust: the virtual team creates this right at the start and falls apart rapidly without it.

Studies of virtual teams have found them doing a wide range of projects: planning a conference, editing a book, offering coordinated service support, developing software, and even starting a company. They rely on telephones, email and sometimes videoconferencing. A few use more sophisticated technology including satellite links and broadband communications.

Virtual teams may combine for one project then disband. They may differ widely in purpose and size, from two or three people to over 100. Few are totally virtual and most have some face-to-face meetings. Their dynamics compare to those of normal teams with a broadly similar team cycle.

CONVENTIONAL TEAMS	VIRTUAL TEAMS
Consistent central core remain	Constantly changing
From same organisation	Possibly from outside organisations (e.g. clients or suppliers)
Dedicated 100% to the team	Attached to several teams
In close proximity to each other	Dispersed across organisation, time, geography
Managed by a single manager	Multiple relationships at different times
Teams have a fixed starting and end point	Teams form and reform continuously
Technology necessary for communications	Technology essential for communications
Trust between members built up slowly	Fragile trust established from the start

The traditional signs of a vibrant team can be elusive or at best ambiguous with a virtual one. For example, in a normal team assessing the performance of individual members and how they are feeling may be relatively straightforward. In a virtual team you may even find it hard to contact people when you need them.

MAKING IT WORK

Two reassuringly familiar leadership signposts remain in this new territory:

- Work happens through relationships. Without these no virtual team succeeds, even though the technology may sometimes appear to bypass this traditional aspect of teamwork.
- It is even more important to invest in proper team development. There may be superb technology and huge databases of information, yet these are only enablers. They are no substitutes for effective team leadership and investing in team processes.

You also still face familiar choices between:

- Top-down and self-organisation.
- Individual and collaborative work.
- Work defined by manager or the team.
- Who gets to do what job.

The issue is not so much how you manage remote teams, it is how you support collaborative working.

Your virtual team still needs to experience the development cycle shown on page 81, even though some stages may be faster or in some cases slower. A BP Amoco project, for example, investigated how virtual teams' performance could be improved and identified slightly different phases of a virtual project: starting, bonding, managing, meeting, working, sharing, tracking, adjusting and closing.

As described in Chapter 6, bonding happens partly in the sorting stage and is critical to a virtual team's success, far more so than for a conventional one.

RECRUITMENT

While recruitment plays a crucial role when establishing any effective team, virtual workers demand special consideration. Naturally, they need to be extremely self-reliant. The team leader may be readily available at the end of a phone or by email, but there will be no chance of popping into the office for a chat or discussing problems in the coffee lounge. Virtual members therefore need to be people who are able to handle difficulties without having the leader as a readily available sounding board.

Virtual team members need to fend for themselves in creating support networks in their location. They also have to be willing to communicate and be enthusiastic about it. As a senior virtual team leader in an international bank commented: 'The main thing I need from my team is to be warned of any problems that are on the horizon.'

Virtual team members are often unsupervised compared to when people work near to each other. So there must be people in the team who actively seek timely communication with the leader. It also helps if they can distinguish between what information to pass on and what is less important.

TRUST

66 If we are to enjoy the efficiencies of and other benefits of the virtual organisation, we will have to rediscover how to run organisations based more on trust than control. Virtuality requires trust to make it work. **99** (Charles Handy)

Trust is pivotal to the virtual team. Without it people simply won't do the work and distance alone soon undermines effectiveness. Yet how is trust created? Is it even possible in a global team without a common past or future, culturally diverse and geographically dispersed and reliant on electronic communication?

In normal teams trust evolves through the stages of initial fear, getting to know you, predicting each other's behaviour, on to empathy and shared values. In a virtual team trust cannot rely mainly on interpersonal relationships since there is seldom enough time to create them. While in romantic relationships absence makes the heart grow fonder, in a virtual team absence can in fact make the heart go yonder.

Research reveals that effective virtual teams generate 'swift trust', which happens right at the start – or not at all. 'You can never give a second first impression' really seems to be true with this kind of team.

So in the early stages of your virtual team make sure there is enough time for establishing trust. In a study of 29 global virtual teams, for example, the first interactions between members were crucial to building trust. Initial communications set the tone for how people related for the entire project. Those teams that failed to become strongly focused in communication about the task had low levels of trust at the end of the project. One team leader whose group never gelled sent an introductory message implying his suspicion of the members' commitment. Another team established a strict set of operational rules but could not move beyond this to an empowering level of trust.

Apart from almost instant virtual teams that combine for a few days or even hours to work on a problem, insist that everyone has a chance to meet each other face to face. If enough is at stake, the resulting increased commitment and trust are a sound investment.

Be willing to spend money to bring the team together. For example, Carrier Corporation could not do this easily on a permanent basis for one group working on a new air conditioner. So it compensated by liberal team training at the project's outset, spending generously on travel for everyone and booking eight hours of videoconferencing time every week for the duration of the project.

Some leaders bring their virtual team together every six weeks, rotating the location between countries and giving everyone a chance to see colleagues in their own environment and to understand what makes them tick.

Tackle communication delays arising from a mix of multiple time zones, busy team members and electronic technology. For example, establish group norms that requests for information will be acknowledged within 24 or 48 hours.

RECOGNITION

Studies of virtual teams show that individual recognition tends to be rather infrequent and conducted through email or a phone call. Some people felt that online recognition was helpful, while others were uncomfortable with it believing that communications should be done in person. Responding to this one team leader arranged a voice conference call to make her praise public and ensure that everyone heard it.

Although recognition could be a raise, promotion or stock options, it is often just enough to say a simple 'thank you' in public. In Maynard Leigh Associates, any network team member can publicly nominate someone for an 'Emily'. There is no physical Emily or even a gift; it is simply a public acknowledgement via email of an exceptional piece of team work.

Because managing from a distance is tricky it can be tempting to use technology for unpleasant tasks such as criticising someone or even sacking them. If you are contemplating remote firing by email, fax or voicemail, don't. Apart from being bad practice and ignoring human sensibilities, it may have serious legal implications.

COACHING

Coaching is a powerful way to support change behaviours and facilitate working as a virtual team. For example, coaching sessions may help people see the bigger picture so that they realise how their work relates to business goals. Similarly, it may be sensible to show people how to get the best results from the technology. Once people understand these resources they also need help gaining the confidence to use them.

BP sponsored research into virtual teams in 1994, introducing desktop videoconferencing tools linked to electronic whiteboards. These allowed people to see the same documents, spreadsheets and diagrams in different locations and to work on them simultaneously. Scanners and Lotus Notes further supported collaboration across time zones and locations. An important part of the process was behavioural coaching designed to help staff handle new ways of sharing and collaborating.

A good coach can also usefully challenge the team's thinking and observe its culture close up. This may lead to noticing what others have missed and perhaps point to behavioural changes that will benefit everyone.

CULTURE

Managing and influencing culture lie at the heart of leading an effective virtual team. Here culture has two distinct aspects:

- Corporate and team culture.
- National culture and diversity.

CORPORATE AND TEAM CULTURE

The leadership challenge is to to influence the virtual team so that it adequately reflects the corporate culture in its work. Since some members of the team may not even be employees of your company, affecting team culture demands a strong mix of ingenuity and persistence.

Virtual teams are 'live', not merely electronic representations of the real thing. So the characteristics of virtuality need to be deliberately built into their culture, including dispersal, empowerment, restlessness, independence, technology, shared purpose and trust. Without these you cannot expect the virtual team to thrive.

In ordinary teams the leader has considerable power, although constrained by factors such as the environment, customers, suppliers and so on. In a virtual team your power is further limited by 'free spirits' doing their own thing, and others taking responsibilities not even assigned to them. Here the effective leader is someone open to losing power, and this can be challenging without suitable coaching or training.

66 Virtual leadership is about keeping everyone focused, as old structures, including old hierarchies, crumble. 99
(Warren Bennis, US leadership expert)

In all types of teams the members act both as individuals and as part of the group. But in a virtual team there is a pronounced emphasis on individuality because often the formal leader is absent. So the team has to develop a culture in which it is mainly self-managing. This is only possible when there is a clear sense of purpose and personal commitment to the group.

What makes the virtual team different from a regular team is unambiguous purpose and the need to keep everyone aligned around it when they can no longer meet together in person. Without the usual relationship-building opportunities the team has to invest in more frequent and explicit check-ins around purpose.

And while leadership in an ordinary team moves around to some extent, in a virtual one this happens constantly. Participating in a virtual team can therefore be a rollercoaster ride of people taking on sudden leadership roles and then passing them on as new expertise comes in to play.

Watch a virtual team at work and you see that people often change roles because the entire process is so dynamic. Tasks alter rapidly, placing a premium on sustained clarity of purpose and mutual trust. Some companies, such as Tetra Pak, have simply abandoned functional divisions, working instead in boundary-crossing networks.

NATIONAL CULTURE AND DIVERSITY

When a virtual team operates across different countries and business backgrounds, people need an understanding of one another's culture. For example, in a global team people must become acquainted with their own and others' attitudes as a step on the route to achieving a common vision.

Both you and the other team members may also need to take into account the local cultures in which particular members works. Being sensitive to diversity issues demands both knowledge of local conditions and patience, since cultural differences may affect how people respond to work requests, criticism, invitations to 'say what you think', work rates and interpretations of terminology.

What is important is no longer the dos and don'ts of an overseas assignment. Instead the shift of focus in the team is towards understanding culture from a collaborative viewpoint. Here the role of the team leader becomes the champion of collaboration, constantly seeking to promote it.

Cultural issues to focus on include:

● What is the team culture?
● How can it be defined and established?
● What is the local prevailing culture and how will it affect behaviours?
● Will the environment support relationships, not just information exchange?
● Do people get the big picture and develop relevant expectations?
● What norms, styles and behaviours will help or hinder the atmosphere you want?

Virtual team members need to be culturally intelligent. They often need to have a dual cultural focus: they must understand the culture of the parent organisation, and at the same time relate to the local culture. In many ways they are cultural interpreters, helping one understand the other.

Oxford based Electrocomponents is a mail order service with teams handling supplies from Singapore, Hong Kong, Australia and Europe. General manager Edward Dowling argues that intercultural training provides the key to making his global teams successful: 'So they can understand the nuances of dealing with someone on the other side of the world.'

Management styles need to be sensitive to national characteristics. One manager adopted a hands-off, empowering approach that was alien to a French colleague reared on command and control. Terse emails led up to an explosion when they met. Similarly, brainstorming sessions may work well with US and UK managers but Scandinavians and Asians may be less voluble and tend to sit quietly, making it hard to judge whether they agree or disagree.

There is, of course, always a danger of stereotyping people according to different cultures. All generalisations of this kind are of limited value. But recognisable differences do exist that reflect particular traditions of education, practices and culture. The culturally intelligent team member needs to learn and adapt quickly to local business customs.

UNDERSTANDING TEAM MEMBERS' LOCAL CULTURE

- Rotate meetings so that you draw in the different countries and their cultures – take a tour.
- When you meet, get each team member to bring in a food item that is distinctive to their culture – have a food tasting.
- Bring in music characteristic of the local culture.
- Ask each person to make a short video of their workplace.
- Learn one another's national flags.
- Teach one another essential phrases from the language.
- Describe a typical Sunday lunch; night out in the local town; adverts on local TV; business outfit etc.

COMMUNICATION

Communication puts a great strain on virtual teams as they attempt to interact, share meaning and reach consensus, all without the rich information from face-to-face contact. Such teams are most successful when they use:

● A wide range of communication tools, not just one narrow group such as the phone or email.
● Technologies that allow members to communicate instantly, which enable collaborative brainstorming, planning and decision making.

THE TECHNOLOGY OF VIRTUAL TEAMS

Your virtual team will rely on better, faster and more imaginative ways of communicating than those used by conventional teams. This is only partly the role of technology. People's expectations differ in a virtual team. They want frequent and regular short interactions rather than longer ones that happen less often. People will therefore look to you to create opportunities for these interactions.

> 3Com, a networking company with employees around the globe, prefers telephone conferencing to videoconferencing. There are fewer distractions, it is quicker to set up and people take more care to talk through visuals. Graphics are emailed to team members in advance of 'meetings'. They look at the documents on their computers while participating in the telephone conference and make changes on screen.

It may require some ingenuity to overcome the location and time zone difficulties inherent in the virtual team. Email can be useful for semi-social chatting while other strategies may be beneficial, such as regular seminars or training days for dispersed staff. You can set up 'follow-the-sun' technologies that kick into action according to local time zones.

Careful use of email and voicemail distribution groups can be extremely useful. It allows team members to communicate with several people at the click of a button. Thus one leader of a high-tech virtual team regularly updates his team with 30-second 'sound bites'. Others in the team are able to provide similar short, sharp exchanges of information.

NCR Corporation devised the Worm Hole, a continuously available audio, video and data link. It supported a virtual team of people working over more than 11 months in three locations developing a next-generation computer system. In the world of the Worm Hole even the grain on the conference tables matched in the three different locations. Whenever members of the virtual team wanted to meet they entered the Worm Hole and instantly connected with each other.

In BP Amoco's Moving Work to People project NCR's Worm Hole concept was extended to include Teamcam, where every virtual team member's computer was equipped with an inexpensive webcam.

Every two minutes an image is uploaded from each camera to a web server. A web page for the whole team combines all these images so that anyone visiting the page sees the latest image from the camera. Like the Worm Hole, this allows people to have a 'meeting' any time they want. With the high resolution and real-time performance of continuously open leased lines, the effect is said to be just like 'being there'.

If you come from an IT background, be aware that you may be more interested in the technology that supports the virtual team than in the team itself! Storing and exchanging data is important, yet what really matters is conversations between team members. This is what you need to support as a team leader and this should be the focus of your technology concerns.

It is the changes in the nature of teams, not in the technology, that create new challenges for team leaders and members. Managing a virtual team means managing the whole spectrum of communication strategies, project management techniques and human and social processes that support it.

You may spend part of your leadership time eliminating glitches in cyberspace that undermine the team's communications. For example in one study, the

---

TECHNOLOGY FOR VIRTUAL TEAMS

- Multimedia PCs
- Mobile phones
- Laptops with communications links
- Desktop videoconferencing
- Application sharing
- Shared electronic whiteboards
- Document scanners
- Internet/intranets
- Groupware
- Rapid file transfer
- Broadband
- Dedicated lines
- Satellite uplinks

Mexican internet server rejected emails from team members in the US, the French server accepted emails but didn't deliver them to the project leader, and teams using web-based collaborative tools couldn't access chatrooms, preventing viable team meetings.

A particular trap to watch out for is assuming that the technology can provide for the less tangible needs of human beings – to keep in touch, to build relationships – just because it enables them to communicate with each other. For example, virtual meeting experiences can be frustrating and disappointing. People may complain of information overload, topic drift or useless conversations. When face-to-face encounters fail we question the design of the meeting. With groupware we tend to blame the technology. Instead, we need to become more aware of group dynamics and understand what happens when people interact with new media.

At the end of each week, rather than asking 'Is the technology working?' try 'Is the communication still interesting and engaging, or has it become stale?'

There is no substitute for face-to-face contact. Without this the team may lack a 'soul' and people may feel it is unreal and hard to identify with. Around 70–80 per cent

of human communication lies in behaviour not words.
Many problems only get resolved in live groups and
dispersed teams cannot afford to lose this benefit.

Steve Pritchard has 25 photographs of colleagues on
his wall. As principal consultant at Transnational
Management Associates he works with virtual teams
running programmes in the US, Europe and Singapore.
The photos reminds him that he is working with people,
not just a voice on the end of a phone: 'It's essential to
have face-to-face contact at the start. It may cost
money but the investment pays huge dividends when
the inevitable problems arise. You have a bank account
of goodwill which can be used to steer the team
members through the potential difficulties of working in
a remote environment.'

ICL's Ian Hardacre runs a pan-European consultancy
operating in Finland, Denmark, the Netherlands, Ireland
and the UK. 'I would never give orders via an email, it is
too inhuman,' he says. 'The way an email is interpreted
depends on the mood of the reader when it arrives. The
sender might keep the message brief, but the tone
could come across curt or unfriendly.'

Good communication is therefore at the heart of managing
and empowering dispersed virtual teams. It is also
important in managing restlessness and independence.

It is worthwhile as well being alert to how
communications can easily go awry. The Human
Communication Research Centre at Glasgow University
found that poking fun at a virtual team can be easily
misinterpreted and special care has to be taken when
humour is directed at individuals.

CONTROL

If you revel in command and control as a management
style, a virtual team will be a shock. Some of your team
may not be directly accountable to you or may even work

for a different organisation. The whole point of a virtual team is that it brings together the essential people, regardless of where they are located.

Virtual teams almost force your management style to switch towards a facilitating mode, since directing or delegating does not work particularly well. As a facilitator you need to pay attention to what is happening in your group, as distinct from what you wanted or expected would happen.

For example, you need to remember everything you have learned about managing and facilitating group processes. Being a leader now means asking yourself 'How can we move these virtual chairs into a circle so that everyone feels involved?' Key ideas to use here are:

● Teamwork is a social activity and depends on relationships.
● Knowledge is built into the team and needs to be made explicit.
● It is important to create ways for team players to experience membership.
● People gain knowledge from observation and experience.
● When people feel engagement they also feel empowered.
● Failure to perform often stems from being excluded from the process.

You may need to develop new approaches to handling accountabilities, decision making and performance management. For example, agreement on who is accountable for what may include:

● *Scope*: what are the timescale and boundaries of responsibility?
● *Exclusions*: when do you need to refer to a superior and who is this?
● *Performance*: what are the overall objectives and background assumptions against which individual and

team results will be judged?

● *Work methods*: rather than unwritten rules, what are the expectations about how people will work together?

The more dispersed the team, the more important it becomes to have clearly defined accountabilities. This is because remote members are more likely to take on responsibilities and the safety net is stronger when team members work in close proximity.

The nature of a virtual team is that people take risks working on their own while contributing to the overall purpose. Consequently they will only perform well when they have the freedom to make mistakes and feel they work in a blame-free culture. Your job of creating such an environment can be challenging if you are used to more traditional ways of leading.

Luckily, you won't even know of the mistakes if you let go of the detail and allow the team to operate organically. Trying to control everything merely ends up affecting people's commitment, far more than in a traditional group.

According to BP's experience, virtual team members who don't know each other well can benefit from a rigorous After Action review that explores:

● What was supposed to have happened?
● What actually happened?
● Why are they different?
● What is the learning?

The review can be done after every event, at the end of the day or a meeting.

You soon learn to judge on results, rather than by monitoring how much effort is being used. Instead of a typical team leadership question such as 'Why did you do that?' you may need to shift to asking:

- What is going on?
- Have I understood what is happened?
- What has been the result?

Measuring a virtual team's performance can be hard. You may need to tailor key performance indicators to fit each part of the team, and these may require regular updating to reflect the restless, organic nature of the virtual team.

Managing a virtual team requires sensitivity. Most members of the group will be experts who survive by their own ability, rather than your grace. You must therefore appeal to mutual interest and your clout comes from knowing things that everyone else would like to know.

KNOWLEDGE MANAGEMENT

The technology used by virtual teams produces enormous flows of information. Consequently in virtual teams as in other areas, knowledge management has become a new discipline in its own right as companies try to make the most of their intellectual capital.

Most virtual teams are only as good as their knowledge base and ability to learn. They rely on rapid access to new and better information, about what works and what doesn't and about who can help and who is available.

Technology enables sophisticated forms of knowledge management as well as better and faster communication. Some of the most valuable work occurs when you help everyone in the team share knowledge and learning. This could mean, for example, creating planned sessions where people talk about their experiences using electronic chatrooms, video and phone conferencing and so on. Or it could mean you spend time ensuring that each person in the team knows how to make the best of the company's intranet facilities.

Another area for your attention is the pace imposed by the technology. Its sheer speed can overwhelm people, particular if some members of the team log on

> BP Amoco's Connect system generates informal knowledge and expertise to create a spiral of help. For example, a manager in South Africa wanted to close a deal selling industrial lubricants to a brewery chain in Tanzania. He searched Connect for people with relevant knowledge and to his surprise found help from staff who had just developed a bid for a Scottish brewery in Aberdeen.
>
> Connect aims to generate 10-minute phone calls and email help requests that can save thousands of dollars by avoiding 'wheel reinvention'. Some 16,000 people have joined the system.
>
> Everyone at BP has the authority and capability to create a web page for the corporate intranet. There are Yellow Pages of in-company experts and BP encourages its people to list their interests, expertise and experiences. It estimates that knowledge sharing through virtual teams saved $30 million in the first year.

four times a day to enter material. This may prove too fast for some people and you may need to take action to slow down the pace:

- Select technology that gives users more capabilities than they currently have. Otherwise why should they feel they are learning?
- Make the technology convenient to access and located where the work gets done.
- Provide quality service and support.

It is harder to share and exploit knowledge in a dispersed team when there is an increased risk of knowledge hoarding and duplication, leading to wasted effort. Effective actions you can take here to encourage better knowledge communication are:

- Accept the cost of regular meetings where dispersed team members are brought together.

- Be willing to visit or send a representative to dispersed team members to gather and pass on information.
- Develop videoconferencing facilities and the confidence of people to use them.
- Reward knowledge sharing across the team. GE in the US, for example, regards supporting colleagues and sharing knowledge as criteria for promotion.
- Hold on to team members whose knowledge you value. They may be far more expensive to replace than members of a conventional team.

SHARED PURPOSE

For most team leaders virtual teams are definitely uncharted territory. Despite all the claimed benefits of such arrangements, those who have to make them work can find it puzzling and difficult. It raises issues such as: How do you get the best from people? What makes it a team anyway? How do you even know when the team is not working well? What does the group do best and what should it avoid doing?

Managing a group of people through technology is definitely different to doing it face to face, or even in the same building. Companies excel when their virtual teams share a common purpose at all levels. Purpose is the glue for virtual teams. By aligning around shared purpose, virtual teams create bonds among their members that are much stronger than those formed in traditional organisations. Once you have a virtual team it must make its purpose and plan explicit in symbols, words, diagrams, tools and handbooks.

☑ Include face-to face time: an initial team gathering and then others periodically to establish ties, relationships and trust and resolve problems

☑ Keep the project visible: this includes overall schedule, progress towards goals, how each member fits in

☑ Keep team members visible: use shared electronic diaries, have a ground rule that when a team member is going out of town others will be notified by email or phone

☑ Enhance text-only communications. Though text is good, it is no substitute for graphics or images for many purposes

☑ Establish ground rules or group norms on how team members interact and what kind of behaviour is accepted. This prevents misunderstandings and disagreements

☑ Take time out for self-assessment: early detection of problems plus action can save the project time and money later

☑ Learn from experience: keep a well-documented project workbook to hand to the next team. Collect data and develop FAQs and other sources that can be shared. For example, store information about what makes a successful videoconference that can help other team members improve theirs

☑ Team members must be clear about purpose, their own role and reporting lines

Have a regular time for communication every week or month. It keeps the team together, regardless of whether there is activity. You have to maintain the rhythm through time and space

 If working across time zones, share the pain. Make sure you rotate meeting times so that everyone has the early or late shift

 Managing a global team is like selling. You have to keep going over the ground constantly to ensure that everyone understands and is up to speed

About the Authors

NLP AT WORK
THE DIFFERENCE THAT MAKES A DIFFERENCE IN BUSINESS
Second edition

SUE KNIGHT

"Sympathetic and clear ... the whole book makes NLP sound reasonable, achievable and commonsense.
If a good visual presentation, jargon-reduced descriptions and lots of examples of NLP at work in the workplace are your desire, this is a great place to start."
NLP World

Neuro   the way you filter and process your experience through your senses
Linguistic   the way you interpret your experience through language
Programming the way you code your language and behavior into your own personal program

Neuro Linguistic Programming is how you make sense of your world and most importantly how to make it what you want it to be. Other books will tell you what to do. The difference that makes a difference with NLP is that it gives you the *how*.

Sue Knight explains the difference that makes the difference between those who excel and those who 'get by' in the way they communicate, motivate, influence, negotiate, lead, empower and manage their own self-development.

This clear and reasonable guide cuts through the jargon of NLP and introduces the techniques that will enable you to:

* become more successful in any area of your life and business that you choose
* choose how you influence the people and situations around you
* improve your ability to learn new ideas
* learn how to generate 100% commitment from yourself and others
* accelerate your progress towards the goals that you set yourself
* manage your emotions so that you can be creative, constructive, influential and understanding
* be sensitive to yourself and others and communicate in a way that others will find compelling and understandable
* tap into your subconscious mind and draw on its superior processing power

Sue Knight is a leading trainer and speaker on NLP for business. She pioneers the special use of NLP to improve the quality of the business world.

UK £14.99, US $19.95
Paperback 1 85788 302 0
390pp 234×189mm

COACHING FOR PERFORMANCE
GROWING PEOPLE, PERFORMANCE AND PURPOSE
Third edition

JOHN WHITMORE

"The book is well structured, well written and practical in a gentle fashion. It is a good model for those wishing to develop their own facilitating and coaching skills. Interesting and topical, it earns credibility by exploring a philosophy of coaching, not insisting on it."
Training and Development

Coaching is now recognized as more positive, effective and empowering than instruction in business, in skill acquisition, in teaching and in sport. Now that coaching is both the tool and essence of company culture change, even the most successful managers are seeking to adapt their style accordingly.

This easy to use handbook will help you learn the skills, and the art, of good coaching and to understand its enormous value in unlocking people's potential to maximize their own performance.

Written by an expert coach, a top performer himself, who now teaches coaching and team-building skills to business and sports people, the book provides the practical skills of coaching and invaluable insights into more effective communication.

The book offers an easy to follow and apply guide to when, where, why, who and how to coach, what the pitfalls are, and the many benefits. It argues persuasively for using questions, rather than instructions and commands, and following the GROW sequence – Goals, Reality, Options, Will – to generate prompt action and peak performance. It explores the dynamics of team development and it positions coaching as the essential team leadership skill.

Clear, concise, hands-on and reader friendly, this is a coaching guide written in a coaching style for business people, sports coaches, parents, teachers, in fact for all those who want to enhance the performance, learning and enjoyment of individuals, of teams – and of themselves.

Sir John Whitmore began his career as a professional racing driver, driving for the highly successful Ford team at Le Mans and winning both the British and European Saloon Car championships in the 1960s. After running businesses in the UK, Switzerland and USA he founded Inner Game Ltd with Timothy Gallwey which has been highly influential in introducing new approaches to sports and business training. John Whitmore consults and lectures widely on coaching and human resource development.

UK £12.99, US $17.95
Paperback 1 85788 303 9
194pp 234×189mm